D0554911

GREAT HISTORIC DISASTERS

THE ATOMIC BOMBINGS OF HIROSHIMA AND NAGASAKI

GREAT HISTORIC DISASTERS

GREAT HISTORIC DISASTERS

THE ATOMIC BOMBINGS OF HIROSHIMA AND NAGASAKI

J. POOLOS

CHELSEA HOUSE
PUBLISHERS

An imprint of Infobase Publishing

THE ATOMIC BOMBINGS OF HIROSHIMA AND NAGASAKI

Chelsea House
An imprint of Infobase Publishing
132 West 31st Street
New York NY 10001

Library of Congress Cataloging-in-Publication Data
Poolos, J. (Jamie)
The Atomic bombings of Hiroshima and Nagasaki / J. Poolos.
    p.   cm.—(Great historic disasters)
Includes bibliographical references and index.
ISBN 978-0-7910-9738-0 (hbk.)
1. Hiroshima-shi (Japan)—History—Bombardment, 1945—Juvenile literature. 2. Nagasaki-shi (Japan)—History—Bombardment, 1945—Juvenile literature. 3. World War, 1939–1945—Juvenile literature. 4. Atomic bomb—History. I. Title. II. Series.
D767.25.H6P66 2008
940.54'2521954—dc22   2008004953

Chelsea House books are available at special discounts when purchased in bulk quantities for businesses, associations, institutions, or sales promotions. Please call our Special Sales Department in New York at (212) 967-8800 or (800) 322-8755.

You can find Chelsea House on the World Wide Web
at http://www.chelseahouse.com

Text design by Annie O'Donnell
Cover design by Ben Peterson

Printed in the United States of America

Bang KT 10 9 8 7 6 5 4 3 2 1

This book is printed on acid-free paper.

All links and Web addresses were checked and verified to be correct at the time of publication. Because of the dynamic nature of the Web, some addresses and links may have changed since publication and may no longer be valid.

Contents

Every year on August 6, people gather in Hiroshima's Peace Memorial Park (above) to leave flowers and remember the victims of the atomic bombings of the city. One of the few buildings to remain standing was renamed the A-bomb Dome and preserved as a reminder of the damage and destruction caused by the attack.

Introduction: The Site of Destruction

If you walk down the main street in Hiroshima, Japan, today, it is almost impossible to tell that it was ever anything but a peaceful, tranquil city. Automobiles and scooters move over tree-lined streets. Lush gardens line the gently flowing river. Despite a population of more than one million people, residents and visitors create a relaxed but active environment. Modern office buildings are a sign of Japan's thriving economy, as are the many restaurants and shops that dot the downtown area.

Only a few signs of what some historians call the most significant event in modern world history remain. The Hiroshima Peace Park is a place that draws many visitors from all nations. The centerpiece of the park is the remains of a concrete building, one of the few buildings in the city left standing after the most powerful bomb attack ever seen. The blown-out windows and framework of the dome remain as a reminder of what the city looked like in 1945. The building stands as a memorial to the tens of thousands of victims. Each year on August 6, Hiroshima Day, ceremonies are held here to remember these people.

It is hard to believe that fewer than 70 years ago the city lay leveled in its own smoldering waste, with up to 140,000 reported dead by the end of the year. Thankfully, scenes of such horrific destruction have not been seen since. The Hiroshima Peace Park remains as a symbol of the vast lengths to which humankind will go to stop dictators determined to rule the world.

1 Prelude to the Bomb

The story of the atomic bomb begins in a setting as unlikely as any: a man standing at the corner of an intersection, waiting for the traffic light to change. The man was Hungarian-born physicist Dr. Leo Szilard. The place was Southampton Row, in London, England. The time was September 1933. It was while on one of his frequent, ambling walks that Szilard envisioned an atomic chain reaction much like a series of traffic lights all changing to green in rapid sequence, allowing traffic to flow again. Szilard had a playful mind, and thoughts such as these served as both stimuli and entertainment.

Szilard was reminded of a novel he had read shortly before he fled Germany at the time Adolf Hitler was rising to power. The book was *The World Set Free*, written in 1913 by H.G. Wells. In the novel, Wells describes a global nuclear war that lays waste to 200 cities by atomic bombs. Szilard tried to imagine the intense energy created by a nuclear bomb. He had some experience in the theories of superweapons, gained the previous year when he was a researcher at the Kaiser Wilhelm Institute in Berlin, Germany. It was there he studied and worked with the great Albert Einstein, with whom Szilard had collaborated on the invention of a new kind of refrigerator. Szilard admired Einstein for his ability to focus on theory and to avoid the distractions of achievement, unlike another accomplished physicist named Ernest Rutherford. Szilard had learned that, during a recent meeting of scientists, Rutherford had described atomic energy as an insignificant idea with no base in the possible. Rutherford had established his reputation by conducting early experiments that gave physicists new insights into the nature of the atom, and he would later be called "the father of the nuclear age." Yet his claim sparked the playful, competitive fires in Szilard.

Ernest Rutherford

Born in 1871 in New Zealand, Ernest Rutherford is known as the father of the nuclear age. His early work on the orbital theory of the atom was instrumental in physicists' ability to understand the nature of the atom. After completing his studies in his home country, Rutherford was named to the chair of physics at McGill University in Canada, where he completed work that would earn him the 1908 Nobel Prize in Chemistry.

Later, with physicist Niels Bohr, he theorized on the existence of neutrons and their role in holding nuclei together. The pair developed a model of the atom, showing its structure as a nucleus surrounded by orbiting electrons.

His research was instrumental in the advancement of nuclear physics, and his work was both a resource and an inspiration to the physicists who would follow him. In 1914, he was knighted, and in 1931, he was named Baron Rutherford of Nelson, a title he held until his death in 1937.

The young scientist set up a meeting with Lord Rutherford, during which he attempted to prove energy was a feasible product of atoms split by neutron bombardment. Peter Wyden wrote in his book *Day One: Before Hiroshima and After* that Szilard told a friend he was "thrown out of Rutherford's office." But he was not easily defeated, and he loved a challenge. So, he set out to prove Lord Rutherford wrong. He knew it would not be easy and that success would mean a dramatic change to the current views of the universe. After all, the word *atom* comes from the Greek word *atomos*, meaning "a thing that cannot be divided." The very idea of splitting something that by conventional wisdom was unable to be split was far-fetched, to say the least. But Szilard, being a bit eccentric himself, embraced the far-fetched.

With enough money to last him the year, he began to devote his energies to the identification of the element that would be best suited for the task. Szilard disliked routine work, and he tried to hire a scientist to research the 92 elements that at the time were known. No one seemed interested, and the project began to lose momentum. It was not until Szilard moved to the United States in 1939, some six years later, that he resumed serious work on atomic chain reactions.

SCIENTISTS FLEE EUROPE

During the 1930s, the center of theoretical physics was in Europe. Much of the major work in the field was being done at universities in England, Italy, and Germany. The physicists working in Europe frequently visited one another to share ideas, work on theoretical problems, and assist with experiments. But dramatic political changes in Europe brought an abrupt end to all that. With the rapid spread of Nazism in Germany and Fascism in Italy and Hungary, scientists and freethinkers were under attack.

Nazism is the word that describes the political policies practiced by Germany from 1933 to 1945 under Adolf Hitler. These policies persecuted the Jewish peoples of Europe, who

Nazis believed were forming a conspiracy against Germany and, for that matter, all of the Western world. Fascism is a political ideology that popularizes the practices that supposedly serve an entire population rather than individuals. Fascism was championed by Benito Mussolini in Italy from 1922 to 1943. It was also the central issue fueling the Spanish Civil War (1936–1939), which at the time was being won by the Fascists. Both Nazism and Fascism denied an individual's importance and instead sought to make all individuals subservient to the state. Nazism took the concept a step further, placing the individual and state at the feet of the White race.

Many European academics, including physicists, were Jewish. As Hitler's German army began to make advances in Europe, there was no safe place for Jews, and many physicists fled their homes for the safety of neutral European countries in the north or for America. Fearing what many saw as the inevitable union of German Nazism and Italian Fascism, many Italian scientists followed suit. The nucleus of European scientists who for so long had enjoyed the comfort and security of a privileged community where they were free to focus on their work was forced to split, its parts scattered across the Western world. Many of these scientists found refuge in the United States, including the world's most famous physicist, Albert Einstein. At first, this seemed like a blow to the pursuit of science. But in the end it provided some of Europe's top physicists with a new home and therefore made them available to contribute to the invention of the atomic bomb.

AN EXCITING BREAKTHROUGH

One day during the first week of January 1939, the noted Danish physicist Niels Bohr was about to board the *Drottningholm*, a ship that would take him and his family from Copenhagen, Denmark—where he had founded the Institute for Theoretical Physics—to safety in New Jersey, where he would take a temporary post at the Institute for Advanced Study at Princeton.

As Bohr was making last-minute preparations, a physicist on his staff named Otto Frisch barged into his office with wondrous news. He had recently visited his aunt, the noted Jewish physicist Lise Meitner, who had fled Germany and her post at the Kaiser Wilhelm Institute in Berlin for the safety of Sweden. When Frisch arrived for the holiday visit, his aunt showed him a letter from her collaborator, Otto Hahn, a chemist who like Niels Bohr had been a student of Rutherford's. Hahn's letter spoke of the recent experiments he and his new

Dr. Leo Szilard (*above*) was the first scientist to conceive a nuclear chain reaction, a process that was the basis for developing nuclear weapons. Aware of the potential for awesome destruction such weapons posed, Szilard attempted to encourage the U.S. government to refrain from using atomic bombs on civilians.

partner had conducted in Germany, in which they bombarded the element uranium with neutrons. To their surprise, some of the uranium had changed into another element, named barium. These results indicated that he and his associates had quite possibly split the nucleus of an atom. But he could not be certain. In a report he sent to a science journal describing the experiment, he wrote, "We cannot yet bring ourselves to this conclusion which is at variance with all previous experience in nuclear physics." But Frisch and Meitner had a strong feeling about the significance of the experiment. And as Frisch, having rushed back to Copenhagen, recounted the story to Bohr as Bohr was preparing to depart for America, he could not contain his excitement.

Bohr shared in Frisch and Meitner's amazement. Over the course of his voyage at sea, he reworked the calculations of the experiment. According to his findings, there was little doubt that the Germans had split the atom. He recalled that Frisch had called the splitting of the nucleus *fission*, a term he borrowed form the biological term for the splitting of a cell. Perfect, he thought.

EINSTEIN'S LETTER

Shortly after the news of the splitting of the uranium nucleus leaked out over America's shores, scientists began in secret to conduct experiments to verify the work of Hahn and Meitner. Some of the world's brightest and most lauded physicists, such as Eugene Wigner, Edward Teller, and J. Robert Oppenheimer—along with Bohr and Szilard—were caught up in the fervor around this unprecedented breakthrough. At once, they began to spread the word within the greater scientific community. Szilard, Wigner, and Teller formed the "Hungarian conspiracy" and took time out from their efforts to build support within the financial community in order to fund further research. They joined Niels Bohr as he delivered a surprise lecture to a meeting of 50 senior scientists at a conference originally scheduled to present findings on an altogether different topic, low-temperature physics. There, in a lecture hall at George Washington University, Bohr related Hahn's findings to the stunned audience. While Teller proposed the possibility of creating and controlling a chain reaction catalyzed by the splitting of the atom, most of the attendees were focused on the question of confirming that nuclear fission actually released energy. And they wasted no time.

That afternoon, delegates from Johns Hopkins University repeated Hahn's experiment. Later that night, a former student of Bohr's, named Merle Tuve, sent a colleague to his laboratory at the Carnegie Institute's Department of Terrestrial Magnetism to perform an experiment to validate Hahn's findings. Upon hearing the news in his office at the University of California at Berkeley, J. Robert Oppenheimer wrote in a letter to a friend, "The uranium business is unbelievable."

But as momentum developed within the cloistered community of physicists across the country, so did the concern that Nazi Germany would use Hahn's findings to build a nuclear bomb. In fact, many scientists in the United States predicted that the Germans were already further along then they were, and this terrible possibility fueled the urgency with which they worked. Their concern was justified. In April 1939, one of Lord Rutherford's trainees, a physical chemist located in Hamburg, Germany, wrote to Hitler's War Office in Berlin to warn the chancellor of the grave possibilities associated with Hahn's work. The letter stated that it was highly likely that the splitting of the atom would lead to the development of a bomb many times more powerful than conventional bombs and that the first country to make use of this technology would have an unsurpassable advantage over other nations. This letter was shown to Hans Geiger, coinventor of the Geiger counter (a device used to measure radioactivity), whose support for the cause led to high-level meetings with physicists and government officials.

Meanwhile, the physicists in the United States worked feverishly to convince the U.S. government of the immediacy of the issue. Szilard asked that all papers on the progress of nuclear study be withheld from publication, for fear the Germans would learn from them. Szilard's colleague Enrico Fermi was granted a brief audience with a military committee, which thought uranium could be best used as a new source of power for submarines. They sent Fermi away, telling him they would be in touch, yet they distrusted the refugee with the Italian name.

That summer, Szilard was told that the United States Navy was at the time unable to support his research on chain reactions because of restrictions on government contracts. Conceding to the reality that the military would not be a source of research funding, Szilard scratched his head. He was distressed by the Nazi embargo on uranium. The world's other

Leo Szilard

Leo Szilard was a Hungarian-born physicist who is credited with conceiving the nuclear chain reaction. Szilard was born in Budapest, Hungary, on February 11, 1898. He studied with Europe's most notable physicists, including Albert Einstein. In 1933, he fled to London to escape Nazi persecution. In 1938, he moved to New York, where he was hired to conduct research at Columbia University.

In 1939, he and fellow physicist Enrico Fermi conducted a successful experiment using the element uranium to trigger a reaction, that showed significant neutron multiplication and demonstrated that theoretically a nuclear chain reaction was possible. Szilard later wrote, "We turned the switch, saw the significant source of the element was in the Belgian Congo. He determined that it was important to warn the Belgian government not to sell uranium to the Germans. He would have to do this through the president of the United States, Franklin Delano Roosevelt. But how would a little-known scientist such as he get the attention of the president? Roosevelt was certainly too busy for him. But there was one man he knew could get the president's ear: his former teacher and collaborator, Albert Einstein. He also recalled that Einstein was an acquaintance of the queen of Belgium, who was known as Princess Elisabeth of Bavaria years before when she and Einstein had played violin together in a chamber music ensemble. Szilard was sure Einstein would at least listen to his plea.

At the time, Einstein was relaxing at a friend's cottage in Peconic, Long Island. Szilard arranged a meeting, and on

flashes, watched for ten minutes, then switched everything off and went home. That night I knew the world was headed for sorrow."

Prior to the destruction of Hiroshima and Nagasaki, Szilard wrote the Szilard petition, which promoted the cause of demonstrating the atomic bomb to an audience of Japanese military before actually using it. He believed that would be enough to discourage the Japanese from further fighting. In the end, President Truman took the advice of his military advisers and attacked Japan.

After the war, Szilard was so horrified by the atomic bomb that he gave up being a physicist and turned his attention to molecular biology.

the morning of Sunday, July 16, 1939, he and Wigner drove to Long Island in Wigner's Dodge coupe. Unable to locate the property, they asked several locals where the cottage was, but no one had heard of it. Then they happened upon a young boy, whom they asked where they might find Einstein. It seemed

One of many scientists who fled Europe before World War II, Dr. Enrico Fermi *(above)* was a colleague of Leo Szilard's at Columbia University. Working together, they invented the world's first nuclear reactor. Later, Fermi would be an important figure in creating and testing the atom bomb.

everyone knew about the great Einstein, even the boy, who pointed them to Old Grove Road.

On vacation, Einstein greeted the men wearing an undershirt and a pair of rolled-up trousers. When Szilard explained his theory of how a chain reaction could be created, Einstein exclaimed, "I never thought of that!" Immediately, he understood the great significance of such a discovery and agreed to do anything he could to convince the U.S. government of the dangers of allowing the Germans to lead the way in developing the technology from which an atomic bomb could be built. In his book *The Manhattan Project*, Daniel Cohen noted that Szilard wrote, "Einstein was willing to assume responsibility for sounding the alarm even though it was quite possible that the alarm might prove to be a false alarm. The one thing most scientists are really afraid of is to make fools of themselves. Einstein was free from such a fear and this above all is what made his position unique on this occasion."

Though Einstein recognized the importance of sounding the alarm, he was reluctant to trouble the queen of Belgium. At the same time, Wigner questioned the wisdom of sending such a letter to a foreign government. At last, the three conspired to write a letter to Roosevelt. Einstein dictated the letter in German, which Wigner took down in longhand. In the letter, he explained that he understood the brutality of the Nazis and that the United States should take any measures necessary to prohibit them from gathering the world's supply of uranium and developing an atomic bomb.

Still, there was the problem of bringing the message to the president's attention. Even though the United States was not yet directly involved in the war in Europe, the president had his hands full with all that was going on there. Szilard called on an old friend from Berlin, who called an acquaintance named Alexander Sachs, an economist who was a friend of the president and who in the past had advised him on economic policy. Szilard met Sachs, who immediately agreed to lend his assistance. Szilard drafted the final letter, refining Wigner's

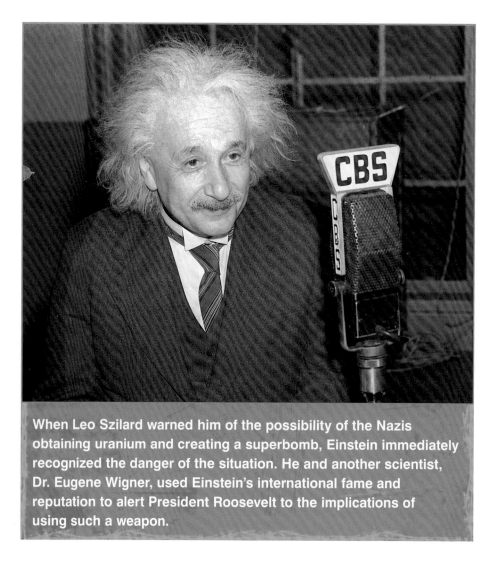

When Leo Szilard warned him of the possibility of the Nazis obtaining uranium and creating a superbomb, Einstein immediately recognized the danger of the situation. He and another scientist, Dr. Eugene Wigner, used Einstein's international fame and reputation to alert President Roosevelt to the implications of using such a weapon.

dictation of Einstein's letter, and on October 11, after Sachs had finally convinced Roosevelt's aides that his news was worth an hour of the president's time, he was led into the Oval Office.

During the weeks leading up to the meeting, Sachs had spent considerable time strategizing his pitch. He knew the meeting was the one chance he would have to convince the president to take action. So when Roosevelt greeted him, he was well prepared. He began by telling the president a story about a young American inventor who had written Napoleon Bonaparte, the great French emperor from 1804 to 1814, with a fresh idea. The inventor knew Napoleon had been unable to invade England because his navy could not solve the tricky tides and currents of the English Channel, which lies between France and England. He proposed a fleet of boats without sails that could attack England in any weather. Napoleon was unimpressed with the idea and dismissed the man. The inventor was Robert Fulton, inventor of the steamboat, which became a commercial success. The story served to warn President Roosevelt that he would be wise to approach the information Sachs had come to bear with an open mind.

In true presidential fashion, Roosevelt handed a note to an aide, who returned a short time later with a rare bottle of Napoleon brandy and two glasses. As the two men sipped the expensive brandy, Sachs presented his own version of the issue, describing the potential uses of nuclear energy and expressing a strong belief that a bomb of untold potential would one day use nuclear fission. In *The Manhattan Project*, Daniel Cohen wrote that Sachs told the president there was no question that one day man would control almost unlimited power. He quoted Sachs as saying, "We cannot prevent [man] from doing so and can only hope that he will not use it exclusively in blowing up his next door neighbor." According to Cohen, Roosevelt grasped the urgency of the issue and responded, "Alex, what you are after is to see that the Nazis don't blow us up. This requires action."

This was the chain of events that led to a government-authorized plan to develop the atomic bomb. After the United States was attacked at Pearl Harbor in 1941, the plan was dubbed the Manhattan Project, named after the New York City borough where early research on the atomic theory had been carried out. The project would cost an estimated $2 billion and contribute not only to the end of World War II (1939–1945) but also to the United States' prominence as a world power for decades to come.

The Origins of War in Europe

World War II was a true world war. Fighting took place all over the globe, on land and on sea. Bloodshed occurred in Asia, Africa, Europe, and in the Middle East. More than 30 million lives were lost. Cities were destroyed, and empires crumbled. As a war, it changed the course of history. As a historical event, it changed the way we think about humankind's capacity to destroy one another.

Rarely are wars caused by a single event. Instead, they are typically the result of a series of events or conditions that collectively lead leaders to perceive their nations are under threat. This was certainly the case with World War II, and to understand the origins of the war, it is helpful to review the events that preceded it during the early part of the twentieth century. In particular, it is important to consider how measures to prevent another major war from happening after World War I actually created conditions ideal for a large-scale, worldwide conflict.

POLITICAL LEFTOVERS

It is easy to see how the war in Europe grew directly from World War I (1914–1918). In what was called "The Great

22

War," the Allied powers of Great Britain, France, Imperial Russia, and the United States defeated the Central powers, led by Austro-Hungarian, Germany, the Ottoman Empire, and Bulgaria. World War I was a global war that wrought devastation, even among the victors. More than 9 million soldiers and civilians lost their lives during the conflict. The war caused the destruction of four world empires: Ottoman, Austria-Hungary, Imperial Russia, and Germany. Following the war, the victors drew up an agreement that disbanded the old world order and, through the Treaty of Versailles, threw Germany into economic ruin.

The treaty, signed on June 28, 1919, marked the official end to the war. But it was not until six months later, at the conclusion of the Paris Peace Conference, that the final details of the agreement between both sides were worked out. The Treaty of Versailles included provisions that required Germany to pay reparations, or damages, to countries it had fought. These provisions were controversial insofar as they served France, who wanted to punish Germany, while ignoring the wishes of Britain, who wanted Germany to remain a strong economic force in order to balance the strong position of the French. The United States simply wanted long-term peace and compensation for its wartime expenditures. President Woodrow Wilson thought Germany should be punished, but he believed too harsh a punishment would push the Germans into rebellion and a possible second world war. Wilson's point of view would prove insightful over the years to come.

The Germans were outraged at the agreement. They felt they had neither started the war nor lost it. They understood the Paris Peace Conference as a peace conference, not as an act of surrender. They were so angry with the pressure from other world powers to sign the treaty that they sank their own ships in protest. Top government officials resigned, and the new government, named the Weimar Republic by historians, assumed leadership. Under this governance, Germany was to operate as a liberal democracy. Ultimately, the endeavor failed with the ascent of Adolf Hitler and the Nazi Party.

A WAR OF IDEOLOGIES

World War II was fought for several reasons, including economic and territorial. But from the perspective of all interested parties, the single most important issue at stake for the United States and its Allied partners was the preservation of democratic ideology from the threat of Fascism, an ideology embraced by the Germans, Italians, and Spanish. With a democracy, the power of a nation is spread among elected representatives of the common people. With Fascism, a strong, centralized government controls power. In essence, Fascists believe the good of the state is more important than the good of the individual. They also believe war is a natural characteristic of a prospering nation. Fascists in Germany even went so far as to believe that people with Aryan features, such as the English, Germans, and Scandinavians, are superior to other races, such as Africans and Jews.

Fascism rose from the chaos that engulfed Europe following World War I, particularly among nations whose economies and general way of life had been severely disrupted due to the sanctions imposed by the victors. Many common citizens in Germany, Italy, and Spain craved order and stability, and thus they embraced the organization and security Fascism promised.

MUSSOLINI AND THE QUICK RISE OF FASCISM IN ITALY

While the Nazis were establishing a firm foothold in Germany, a similar dictatorial political movement was gaining momentum in Italy. Italy's economy took a turn for the worse following World War I, and power-hungry politicians seized the opportunity to convince the population that better times lay ahead. As with Germany, political powers in Italy attempted to establish a liberal democracy, but members of the rapidly growing Fascist and Socialist parties resisted their efforts. King Victor Emmanuel III was pressured to choose a political leader from one of these two competing parties. He gave Benito Mussolini, who had risen rapidly through the ranks of the Fascist Party, permission to form a government.

The Fascists used propaganda and intimidation to promote their agenda, which valued nationalism, socialism, and strict adherence to rules. Mussolini's "Blackshirts," a private army of former soldiers, rounded up the dictator's enemies and political opponents, many of whom were murdered. The

Through force and propaganda, Benito Mussolini grew popular with the Italian masses. Given the power to form a new Italian government with his Fascist party, Mussolini *(center)* used a group of former soldiers to strong-arm dissidents and set his sights on domination.

country saw progress, as there were noticeable improvements in industry and civil services, such as the transportation system. But the political corruption that grew out of Fascist Italy was problematic, and rather than solve internal problems, Mussolini looked outside of Italy for new conquests that would cement his popularity.

HITLER AND THE RISE OF NAZISM

Over the next 15 years, while the Weimar Republic attempted to cultivate a fair, democratic government, other German leaders stewed as their country suffered through what they felt were undeserved hardships. In addition to the economic hardships mandated by the Treaty of Versailles, these leaders were angry at the former government for surrendering. They were especially angry with the men who profited from the war by selling weapons and who controlled the availability of weapons to the German army. They believed that the war was theirs to win until the arms dealers cut off their supply of weapons. Many of these weapons dealers were Jewish, and so—along with a history of anti-Semitism—a strong resentment toward all Jewish people began to grow among a faction of these leaders. This was the basis for the rapid rise of the Nazi Party and of the man who would become their leader: Adolf Hitler.

Hitler rose to prominence in the 1920s and was named chancellor in January 1933. He built support among German leaders by playing to their sense of nationalism. He made them believe that if Germany was ever to regain power it would have to do so on its own terms, by the sheer will of its people, who were undoubtedly the most capable in the world. He convinced them that the stronger the national identity, the stronger the nation. Anyone who expressed even the slightest doubt in the superiority of Germany would be pushed aside or eliminated.

He wasted no time exerting his new authority. He began at once to cancel civil and political liberties. By March 1933, he passed the Enabling Act, transferring all legislative powers to

The Brutality of Hitler

Hitler's vision for Germany was centered on a "master race" living in wealth and comfort. At the outset of World War II, he had two goals that would contribute to the realization of this vision: one, to create a racially pure German population, and two, to establish a new home for Germany, expanding its borders into Europe and Russia. As the German army began its campaign to expand its borders, the Nazi Party began its campaign of genocide.

Hitler's quest to cleanse the German race of unsound elements began with a program designed to eliminate Germany's disabled population. As a result, between 75,000 and 250,000 physically and mentally disabled people were killed. Hitler was especially intent on exterminating Jews because he believed they were the root of all evil in the world. Under his direction, the Nazis developed "The Final Solution to the Jewish Question," a plan to systematically exterminate the Jewish population in Europe. By early 1942, the first extermination camps had been built, and Operation Reinhard began. Jewish citizens—men, women, and children—were taken from their homes and shipped by train to concentration camps, where they were shot in groups or led into large rooms filled with poison gas.

Hitler's strongest supporters in this plan and the two men who were credited for managing the Nazi concentration camps met their ends after Germany surrendered. Adolf Eichmann, found hiding in Argentina, was brought to Israel, where he was tried for war crimes and executed. Heinrich Himmler committed suicide when he was captured by the British army near the end of the war.

Hitler's cabinet. He then began to eliminate opposition within the Nazi Party. Anyone who questioned his authority or who supported socialism (in this case, meaning a government that served the people) more than they supported German nationalism (a government that served the interests of German leaders) was killed. In August 1934, when the president of Germany, Paul von Hindenburg, died, Hitler eliminated the office of the president as well as his own post of chancellor. He replaced these offices with a single office, a dictatorship, and declared himself Führer, or leader, of a new order, which he called the Third Reich. With full command of Germany's government and military, Hitler was in prime position to carry out his master plan.

JAPAN BECOMES MILITARISTIC

While Fascism took a foothold in Europe, unrest was brewing on the other side of the world. Traditionally, the Asian powers of China and Japan had resisted Western expansionism. Both countries had long been centers for European trade, offering spices, silk, rice, tea, and other goods for European-made goods such as cloth and machines. Japan saw the threat of European expansion into Asia and adopted a national policy that would ensure its place as a world power.

By the time World War I began, Japan had already begun a program of expansion into a world colonial power. Because the small country had few natural resources, its military leaders believed expansion was necessary even to defend Japan against its longtime enemy, China, as well as the European powers. During World War I, Japan fought on the side of the Allies, which included France, Great Britain, Russia, and the United States. Following the war, Japan's leaders felt that Allied delegations treated them as an inferior country and did not give them the rewards they deserved. They were equally offended in 1922, when the Washington Naval Conference proposed the size of Japan's fleet be smaller than the fleets of Great Britain and the United States. The perceived arrogance of these nations would become an important factor in turning Japan from friend to foe.

Although Japan prospered economically immediately following World War I, the 1923 Tokyo earthquake signaled an abrupt change. The earthquake leveled the capital city, killing some 140,000 people and disrupting services and industries that affected the entire island nation. This natural disaster, coupled with the worldwide economic depression of the 1920s and 1930s, triggered a shift in Japanese politics. While Japan had been working toward establishing a democracy, its military leaders began to gain power within the government. These individuals were too impatient for democracy and felt there should be a government focused on expanding Japanese influence and controlling the raw materials of its neighbors.

In 1931, Japanese troops invaded Manchuria, in northern China. They easily conquered the region and were met with no resistance from the United States, European powers, or the Soviet Union. In 1934, the Japanese government set forth the Amau doctrine, which declared that Japan controlled China and its resources. Japanese military leaders grew bolder and bolder, until in 1937 Japan invaded China itself in an attempt at all-out war. The Japanese Imperial Army quickly built a reputation as barbaric and violent, as it looted and burned the city of Nanjing and raped and murdered its inhabitants in an attempt to intimidate the countries that neighbored Japan from resisting future attacks.

The United States and the United Kingdom turned their attention to supporting China via loans and covert military assistance. They instituted embargoes on raw materials, including oil, hoping to starve Japan of resources. Japan reacted with aggression. It declared war on territories rich in resources, such as the Dutch East Indies, Malaya, and the Philippines. The Japanese felt the Dutch and British governments were too busy with the war in Europe, that the Soviets were stressed by their confrontations with Germany, and that the United States would

Hitler *(left, with German president Paul von Hindenburg)* was able to use his oratorical skills to whip the German public into a frenzy of national and racial pride. When he assumed ultimate power as *Führer*, he began to expand Germany's borders while implementing plans to ethnically cleanse the population of Germany and the rest of Europe.

not be ready for war for some time. Thus, the Japanese began their great expansionist endeavor, the Greater East Asia War in the Pacific, more commonly known as the Pacific War.

HITLER AND MUSSOLINI IN SPAIN

In 1936, at about the time that physicist Leo Szilard took that fateful London walk during which he envisioned an atomic reaction, Spain saw a shift in power when a group of left-wing political parties took over. This progressive group was supported largely by radicals, Communists, and anarchists. The relatively conservative army then rebelled against the country's new leaders. These army rebels were under the command of General Francisco Franco and were supported by Spain's Fascist Party, the Catholic Church, and a large part of the middle class. The result was a civil war between the adherents of two political ideologies of Communism and Fascism.

Hitler and Mussolini, being anti-Communists themselves, saw an opportunity to get involved with the Fascist cause and came to the aid of Franco's Nationalist Party. Hitler sent tanks, aircraft, and 10,000 troops. Mussolini sent 50,000 troops. While Hitler and Mussolini hoped to gain an ally in Franco, they also saw an opportunity to give their armies real-world experience with war as well as to demonstrate the capabilities of the German air force. Of particular note was the bombing of the Basque village of Guernica, which suffered vast civilian casualties and near total destruction. This bombing demonstrated the power of the German air attack as well as Hitler's blatant disregard for civilian life. According to some historians, the air attack on Guernica intimidated Europe's political leaders, who found even more reason to avoid war with Germany and Italy.

GERMAN EXPANSIONISM

Once the Nazis had established a strong foothold among their own people, they turned to the rest of the world. On March 16, 1935, Hitler ordered Germany to rearm. Government arms spending increased by 70 percent, and much of Germany's workforce was put to work producing battleships, submarines, tanks, and warplanes. These acts were in direct violation of the Treaty of Versailles, which mandated that an active German army was forbidden by international law. Hitler's bold move was met with almost no resistance. In fact, the British, sympathetic to Germany's struggle under what they believed were the Treaty of Versailles' too-harsh restrictions, signed the Anglo-German Naval Agreement, authorizing Germany to construct a fleet no larger than one-third the size of the British Royal Navy. The agreement included a provision in which the Royal Navy would cease its operations in the Baltic Sea, effectively handing the territory to Hitler.

Germany immediately moved into the Rhineland and in November 1936 signed the Anti-Comintern Pact with Japan, in which the countries formed an alliance against the Soviet Union and Communism in general. Italy joined the alliance in 1937. Bolstered by the support of Japan and Italy, Hitler found himself in position to expand German influence in Europe. While both Japan and Italy allied with Germany simply to expand their colonial possessions, Hitler had a much grander vision. He wanted Germany to rule the world. In his book *The Causes of World War II*, author Paul Dowswell stated that Hitler believed the execution of a two-stage plan would accomplish German rule. In the first stage, Germany would regain the territories it lost as a result of the Treaty of Versailles as well as expand into Europe. Once Germany controlled eastern and central Europe, it would have plenty of coal, iron ore, oil, and manpower to build a war machine that would allow him to achieve his stage-two goals. In stage two, he would build an empire to the east of Germany for his master race.

In March 1938, German troops marched into Hitler's homeland, Austria. Hitler immediately annexed Austria, making it a province of Germany. Hitler viewed the annexation as a test of Europe's reaction to his violations of post–World

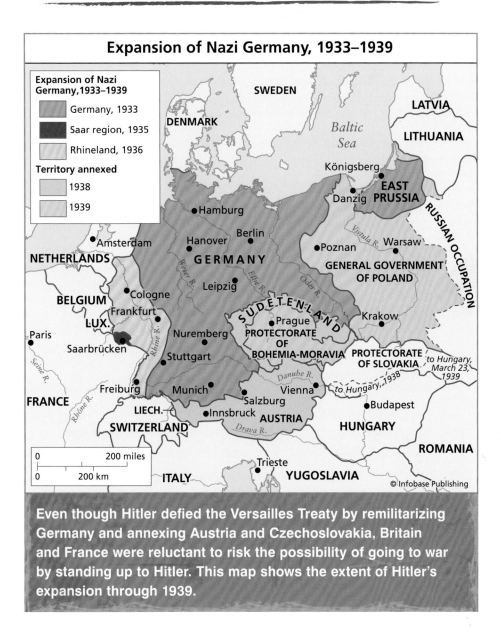

Expansion of Nazi Germany, 1933–1939

Expansion of Nazi Germany,1933–1939

- Germany, 1933
- Saar region, 1935
- Rhineland, 1936

Territory annexed

- 1938
- 1939

SWEDEN

LATVIA

DENMARK

Baltic Sea

LITHUANIA

Königsberg

EAST PRUSSIA

Danzig

• Hamburg

NETHERLANDS

• Amsterdam

Hanover •   Berlin •

GERMANY

Vistula R.   Warsaw

• Poznan

GENERAL GOVERNMENT OF POLAND

Weser R.

Oder R.

RUSSIAN OCCUPATION

BELGIUM

• Cologne

Frankfurt

LUX.

Leipzig •

Elbe R.

S U D E T E N L A N D

• Prague

Krakow •

Paris •

Saarbrücken

Nuremberg •

PROTECTORATE OF BOHEMIA-MORAVIA

Rhine R.

• Freiburg

Stuttgart •

PROTECTORATE OF SLOVAKIA

to Hungary, March 23, 1939

FRANCE

Seine R.

Rhône R.

LIECH.

Munich •

Danube R.

Vienna •

to Hungary, 1938

Salzburg

• Innsbruck

AUSTRIA

• Budapest

SWITZERLAND

Drava R.

HUNGARY

ROMANIA

| 0 | 200 miles |
| 0 | 200 km |

ITALY

Trieste •

YUGOSLAVIA

© Infobase Publishing

Even though Hitler defied the Versailles Treaty by remilitarizing Germany and annexing Austria and Czechoslovakia, Britain and France were reluctant to risk the possibility of going to war by standing up to Hitler. This map shows the extent of Hitler's expansion through 1939.

War II treaties. Sensing the British and the French would not interfere with his aggressive moves, he set his sights on Czechoslovakia, a small country that had alliances to both nations. While France and Great Britain eyed the dictator with reservation after he took Austria, neither country felt the need to intervene. They believed he was "marching in his own backyard" and did not represent a threat to their own plans of colonization. But when Hitler began his plans to invade Czechoslovakia, Europe's two main powers grew concerned.

AN AGREEMENT FOR PEACE

Britain's prime minister, Neville Chamberlain, and France's prime minister, Édouard Daladier, suddenly recognized that Nazi Germany was once again a threat. They wanted to maintain the prestige they had gained as European powers and hold Germany from eating into their share of Europe, but they were ill-prepared to back their policies with force. While Hitler was building a massive army in Germany, their countries were not prepared for war. The awful memories of the slaughter of World War I were still fresh in the minds of their publics, who wanted to avoid another war at all costs. As well, both countries saw Nazi Germany as a potential ally against the Communist Soviet Union. They believed the best course of action was a plan of appeasement, which meant they would allow Germany, which they believed may have been unfairly sanctioned under the Treaty of Versailles, to reclaim the territories it had lost, so long as Germany agreed to expand no farther into Europe.

Chamberlain and Daladier called a meeting with Hitler in Munich, Germany, in September 1938. During this meeting, the parties agreed that Germany was entitled to the Sudetenland, which was the portion of Czechoslovakia that was home to many German-speaking supporters of Hitler. In return, Hitler agreed that Germany would make no additional territorial claims in Europe. This agreement was satisfactory to Chamberlain and Daladier because they could do nothing to stop Hitler from taking the Sudetenland. The agreement was popular among both the British and the French. When Daladier returned from the meeting, he was greeted by a half-million supporters; and Chamberlain in turn was hailed as a hero, claiming triumphantly that he had achieved "peace in our time." But all too soon, events would take a dramatic turn. In March 1939, just a few months after the Munich agreement, Germany marched into Prague, the capital of Czechoslovakia, breaking Hitler's pact with France and Great Britain and setting the world on edge.

Meanwhile, in the United States, Leo Szilard continued to refine his theories. When he was not scribbling figures into notebooks, he was writing letters to colleagues in an attempt to recruit them to join his team. He also kept pressure on the administration to come through with funds to support the research. The fact that he was an ocean away from the conflict did nothing to diminish the urgency of his work.

3 The Conflict Takes Shape

During the 1930s, the mood in the United States was staunchly antiwar. The failure of World War I to create democracy in Europe was in the front of people's minds. In addition, some public opinion held that America had been dragged into World War I by arms manufacturers and business opportunists seeking profits, and no one wanted to repeat that scenario. Consequently, Congress passed a series of acts that prohibited American government and American businesses from selling arms to foreign nations or from lending them money to buy arms. By creating such acts, Congress effectively prevented the United States from getting involved in the Spanish Civil War or from defending Ethiopia from Mussolini's invasion in 1935.

President Franklin Delano Roosevelt understood the antiwar sentiment among Americans. Oceans separated America from Europe, the Soviet Union, and Asia. Natural resources and the means to manufacture them into finished goods were plentiful in the vast country. There was a feeling of isolationism within the country, of wanting to leave the ugly conflicts to other countries while America went about its own business. Respecting this feeling, Roosevelt's public strategy was to isolate

General Information

Allied Powers:
Soviet Union
United States
United Kingdom
China
France

Axis Powers:
Germany
Japan
Italy

Important Leaders
Joseph Stalin: Soviet Union
Franklin Roosevelt: United States
Harry S. Truman: United States
Winston Churchill: Great Britain
Chiang Kai-shek: China
Charles de Gaulle: France
Adolf Hitler: Germany
Hirohito: Japan
Benito Mussolini: Italy

Allied Casualties
Military dead: More than 14 million
Civilian dead: More than 36 million
Total dead: More than 50 million

Axis Casualties
Military dead: More than 8 million
Civilian dead: More than 4 million
Total dead: More than 12 million

Europe's Fascist dictators from the benefit of American trade. Yet even this mild interference with European affairs ruffled the feathers of Americans. All along, Roosevelt knew that at some point the United States would have to rise to the occasion and offer help to the European nations fighting Hitler, but for the time being, he kept the American troops at home and made no public measures to prepare for war.

INTO POLAND

Following Hitler's blatant disregard for the Munich agreement, both Great Britain and France reluctantly began discussions with the Soviet Union about entering into an agreement. Prior to Hitler's invasion of Prague, the English and the French feared the Communist Soviet Union even more than they feared Germany. Both nations mistrusted the Soviets and felt they had little to gain with an alliance. Nonetheless, they began talks with the Soviets in the summer of 1939, only to have the negotiations end when little progress was made. At the same time, Nazi foreign minister Joachim von Ribbentrop initiated discussions with his Soviet counterpart, Vyacheslav Molotov. Molotov knew the Germans planned to invade Poland and was eager to form a productive alliance, despite the difference in the two countries' political ideologies. On August 24, 1939, the nations signed a treaty that stipulated neither would attack the other. As part of the agreement, the Soviets would supply Germany with raw materials in exchange for weapons. Germany would also have control of west Poland, and the Soviets would gain control of Finland, the Baltic States, and east Poland. When Hitler learned the agreement had been reached, he was certain that neither France nor Great Britain would intervene with his planned invasion of Poland. He immediately sent tanks and troops to the border to await his command.

By invading Prague and western Czechoslovakia and flying in the face of the Munich agreement, Hitler humiliated both Britain and France. Yet Hitler had not recognized his

In September 1939, the Soviet Union and Nazi Germany put aside their differences to create a treaty that guaranteed war supplies and territories. Part of this treaty included an agreement that allowed both countries to invade Poland. *Above*, German and Russian officers take part in a ceremony celebrating the new border that ran through Poland and made Germany and the USSR neighbors.

political error in slighting these European powers. They were determined to crush the Nazi dictator at any cost. At the time, the three powers were of about equal military strength. France and Great Britain realized that if Germany were allowed to take Poland, it would be much stronger than them. Both nations had also made agreements with Poland that they would attack Germany if Poland was invaded. Having built up their armies over the year, France and Great Britain were prepared to take measures to stop Germany from additional aggression.

Nonetheless, Hitler read things differently. He believed that the lack of intervention from Europe's great powers when he invaded Prague was an indication of their unwillingness to defend the rest of eastern Europe He was made even more confident by Germany's pact with the Soviet Union. Hitler believed that the power and force of the German army intimidated Europe and France and that neither country would interfere with his plans. On September 1, 1939, German troops poured over the border and into Poland. The news came as no surprise to world leaders, who had long been expecting the volatile Hitler to cross the line with yet another act of unwarranted aggression. On September 3, France and Great Britain declared war on Germany. If Hitler was worried about his young German army butting heads with the world's two greatest empires, he did not show it. The German army rolled through Poland, using its blitzkrieg tactics (precise, swift, and violent military offensives supported by intense aerial attacks). Within a month, Poland was Hitler's.

FRANCE AND GREAT BRITAIN RESPOND

Though neither France nor Great Britain had wanted to engage in war, Hitler's blatant aggression left them little choice. They knew the German dictator would not stop at Poland, and within their respective countries, they intensified preparations for the fight. While some historians argue that even at the time their armies were strong enough to defeat the Germans,

Hitler had so thoroughly convinced the world that his forces were stronger than they were that neither country positioned its armies for battle.

By this time, British prime minister Neville Chamberlain had been pushed out of government in disgrace. The British parliament felt he had greatly mistaken his influence over Hitler and that he was too soft a leader to make the hard decisions that were part of a wartime government. In his place, Winston Churchill stood as the new prime minister. Churchill had long been outspoken about the treatment of Hitler. He felt the German dictator's defiant behavior should have been dealt with earlier. He was a brash, outspoken leader who would become one of the greatest heroes of British history. Churchill was described as a leader whose time had come. Indeed, he realized the time was near when British soldiers would find themselves in battle.

In April 1940, the German army suddenly attacked Norway and Denmark, which were quickly conquered. Then, in what has been described as a military masterpiece, Hitler attacked France. The French had expected Hitler to attack through Belgium. But Hitler outwitted the French military leaders and sent his troops through the Ardennes Forest, which lay farther to the south and was thought to be impassable. French and British armies fought the Germans in Belgium, while larger numbers of Germans poured through the Ardennes and straight into the French capital of Paris. Though the German army was stretched thin at this point, their rapid attack overwhelmed the French. The French government agreed to let Hitler occupy half of France, while they governed the remainder of the country. This was known as the Vichy government, named after the small city of Vichy, which became the new French capital. When the Italian dictator Benito Mussolini joined Hitler, sensing a German victory and eager to share the spoils, French morale sank. Within weeks, France surrendered.

Meanwhile, in the United States, the nuclear project was off to a slow start. But soon after France fell to Germany, the U.S. government finally approved funds for Leo Szilard's research on chain reactions. The experiment Szilard suggested was actually designed by Enrico Fermi. A team of scientists would test Szilard's theories by creating a self-sustaining reaction at the atomic level. Szilard's team began work at once to design and create materials for the experiment.

ROOSEVELT WORRIES

America viewed the events in Europe with alarm. Still, Roosevelt heeded to public opinion and kept the United States out of the war. He was worried about Japan, which he knew wanted to become the most powerful country in Asia and feared would take advantage of the instability in Europe to meet its goals. At this time, Japan's government was being gradually replaced with more aggressive, militaristic leaders. Roosevelt convinced Congress to authorize a large sum of money to double the navy and to pass the Selective Training and Service Act, which would allow men to be drafted into the military. He also offered Great Britain the Lend-Lease program, whereby the United States loaned the British 50 retired navy destroyers in exchange for a lease on naval bases in the Caribbean Sea. In short, he prepared America for war and lent assistance to Great Britain without actually entering the war. Meanwhile, in September 1940, Japan signed an alliance with Germany and Italy, creating the Axis powers that would come to be the collective enemy of the Allies. This worried Roosevelt even more. Hitler had proven to be much more than a mere nuisance in Europe, but Japan was the greater immediate threat to America. In fact, by the spring of 1941, U.S. intelligence had learned that Japan was planning an attack in the Pacific sometime after mid-November. Exactly where and when they did not know.

THE U.S. UNDER ATTACK

On the morning of December 7, 1941, minutes before 8:00, hundreds of Japanese planes, launched from aircraft carriers at sea, attacked Pearl Harbor, a naval base in Honolulu, Hawaii. While the planes dropped bombs and shot up the naval base and the many ships at dock, Japanese submarines crept into Pearl Harbor and fired torpedoes at the defenseless American ships. Caught off guard, the Americans offered little resistance. Within two hours, airports, supply depots, and hundreds of American airplanes were destroyed. Eight battleships were sunk or severely damaged, and 2,403 Americans were dead. It was

The U.S. military was unprepared and overwhelmed when a swarm of Japanese aircraft filled the sky above Pearl Harbor on December 7, 1941, and destroyed much of the U.S. naval fleet stationed there. The next day, President Franklin Delano Roosevelt addressed Congress with a declaration of war against the Axis powers and referred to the attack on Pearl Harbor as "a day that will live in infamy."

a devastating loss for the American navy, and the attack sent shock waves through the public that are still felt to this day.

The United States immediately declared war on the Axis powers—Germany, Italy, and Japan. Pearl Harbor brought the horrors of the war home, and the American people were forced to recognize the reality of the situation: They would have to fight back. Considering the U.S. military was unprepared to enter the war, there was a lot of work to do. Once

Just How Surprising Was Pearl Harbor?

Ever since the 1930s, when the United States imposed trade embargoes on Japan to discourage the Asian nation from continuing its aggressive expansion into Manchuria and French Indochina, tensions began to build between the two countries. Wary of a possible attack, the U.S. Navy had in place a plan to defend its westernmost bases, including Pearl Harbor. Why, then, were the Americans unprepared for Japan's attack?

U.S. military intelligence indicated a growing hostility in Japan toward America. Even the American newspapers carried stories about the escalation of tensions between the two countries. In late November, Pacific commands were warned explicitly that Japan was expected to attack any day. Why did the navy not try harder to protect Pearl Harbor?

At about 7:00 A.M. on the morning of December 7, 1941, two radar operators noticed an unusually large blip on their radar screen. When they called headquarters to report their findings, they were told not to worry. Why did military the United States officially entered the war, the Germans aggressively attacked U.S. shipping. German submarines, with no resistance, patrolled the Atlantic coast within sight of land. In 1942, they sank 8 U.S. ships in a 12-hour period in New York Harbor. The Germans also attacked U.S. freight ships, interrupting the supply of goods destined for Europe. By June 1942, the Germans had sunk some 4.7 million tons of shipping.

personnel at headquarters not investigate the report? Why were sailors sleeping in their quarters or eating breakfast? Why were the guns left unmanned?

Some historians have suggested the United States Navy believed Japan would attack U.S. interests in the western Pacific and that Pearl Harbor would be safe. But others believe the navy was well aware that the Japanese would attack Pearl Harbor and that they kept their knowledge of the attack a secret. Why would they do such a thing? At the time, America was on the verge of war. President Roosevelt knew it would be only a matter of time before the Americans would involve themselves in the war. He was ready to send American forces to Europe to fight Hitler, but he had little support from the American public. An attack on American soil might be just the thing to help Americans see his point of view and speed America's entry into the war.

Because there is little conclusive evidence of this or other theories, we may never know if U.S. military intelligence, or Roosevelt himself, had been forewarned of the attack on Pearl Harbor.

In the midst of all this chaos, Szilard and his team of scientists worked in secrecy. On December 2, 1942, they carried out the experiment that demonstrated the basic principle of a self-sustaining chain reaction. (This event is described in detail in Chapter 6.) The physicists were well on their way to the next step in the development of the atomic bomb.

4. The War in Europe

A s a result of the devastating attack on Pearl Harbor, the United States began manufacturing fast ships that were effective in combating submarines. Strategies for transporting goods were also modified so that ships traveled in large groups, or convoys, escorted by destroyers that could defend the freighters against attack from the sea and air. These measures proved successful at protecting ships and also at sinking German submarines. As the German navy suffered submarine losses, it pulled back in order to protect its fleet.

Meanwhile, the Allies—the United States, Great Britain, France, and Russia—knew that an all-out assault on the Germans to recover France was necessary. Roosevelt and Churchill agreed that France took priority over Japan. First, the Allies would need to suppress German threats in other areas of the Western world. At this point, the British were fighting the Italians in the North African deserts, and the Russians were busy defending their border against the Germans. Stalin, too, wanted the Allied troops to attack France in order to relieve the pressure from the Russian front, but Allied commanders decided that the first priority was to run the Germans out of North Africa. If the Allies controlled North Africa, the Germans would not be able to retreat in that direction once the Allies began pressuring them from western Europe, and the Germans would not be able to access oil and other supplies from Africa and the Middle East. Most important, the British would retain control of southern Europe, the Mediterranean Sea, and the Suez Canal, which was immensely important to transportation lines between Britain, India, and Australia. Allied commanders devised a plan that called for American troops to assist the British in taking back North Africa. Once North Africa was secure, the Allied troops would move north into Europe.

THE DESERT WAR

The North African Campaign of World War II, more commonly known as the Desert War, took place in the desert of North Africa. It began in June 1940 and ended in May 1943. On September 13, 1940, 200,000 Italian troops invaded Egypt, which at the time was held by the British. As the Italians set up a defense before moving inland to capture more territory, the Allies launched a counterattack, designated Operation Compass. The British Western Desert Force marched across Libya, fighting the Italians along the way. Although they were outnumbered 200,000 to 35,000, they surprised the Italian army, which surrendered in its entirety. It was the first official battle in the North Africa campaign and a stunning victory for the British Western Desert Force.

The military action created a front at Al-Agheila, a coastal city at the bottom of the Gulf of Sidra. As the British Western Desert Force sent most of its soldiers to retake Greece from the Germans and Italians, word of its phenomenal victory over the Italians reached Germany. Hitler immediately sent reinforcements to aid the Italians. Field marshal Erwin Rommel and the Deutsches Afrikakorps (German Africa Corps) arrived to rescue to the Italians. Nicknamed the "Desert Fox" for his cunning strategies in tank warfare, Rommel was a shrewd commander. Ordered to hold his position at Al-Agheila, he saw the opportunity to exploit the British position, and he recaptured the ground the Italians had lost during Operation Compass. As a result of the arrival of the Deutsches Afrikakorps, the Allies sent the British Eighth Army, a multinational collection of troops from Australia, New Zealand, India, and South Africa, to fight the German forces. These forces were led by General Bernard Montgomery. Over the next two years, Montgomery and Rommel engaged in a battle of wits in the North African desert.

THE MANHATTAN PROJECT FINDS A NEW HOME

The year 1942 saw dramatic changes for the atomic bomb program, which in 1941 had been given the name the Manhattan Project. Up until that point, the physicists had organized the work. But the U.S. Army thought it was time to step in to run things and make sure the work got done efficiently and with a minimal risk of espionage. The army appointed General Leslie Groves as the director of the operation. Knowing nothing about physics or, for that matter, scientists, Groves immediately began a search for a go-between, someone who could manage the physicists while he took care of logistics. Groves hired Robert Oppenheimer, a wiry, young physicist with a reputation for unusual brilliance. Groves knew Oppenheimer was knowledgeable about all scientific aspects of the project and that he would be the glue to hold it all together. More important, Oppenheimer had the respect of the other scientists.

During the autumn of 1942, Groves and Oppenheimer led a team of army personnel in search of a suitable spot for the Manhattan Project. They needed a wide-open space, preferably on a hilltop so the area could be easily protected from intruders or attacks. It had to be far enough away from towns, just in case something went wrong and to maintain secrecy. After weeks of searching remote areas of New Mexico, Oppenheimer suggested they visit a place he had known as a boy.

The Los Alamos Ranch Boys' School was a school whose mission was to toughen up city boys. Oppenheimer, who had suffered various ailments as a child, was sent to the school as a youngster to build up his strength. Groves found the site far more suitable than the others they had looked at. The school

General Leslie Groves *(right)*, an Army engineer who had just finished supervising construction of the Pentagon, was appointed as head of the Manhattan Project. He hired Dr. J. Robert Oppenheimer *(left)* as the scientific director of the team, and the two made an unlikely pairing that bore fruitful results.

J. Robert Oppenheimer

Robert Oppenheimer was a U.S.-born physicist who is best known for his role as director of the Manhattan Project. As a student at Harvard, he majored in chemistry but, unlike most scientists, immersed himself in a number of widely varying disciplines, including architecture, art, classic literature, and Greek. After graduating summa cum laude in three years, he traveled to Europe to study physics, earning a Ph.D. at 22 years of age. During the course of his academic work, he published more than a dozen important articles that contributed to the emerging field of quantum theory.

General Leslie Groves took a gamble when he hired Oppenheimer to direct the Manhattan Project, for Oppenheimer had past links to the Communist Party. His mastery of the various scientific aspects of the project made him, really, the only man for the job. In fact, the entire period Oppenheimer was in Los Alamos, he was under investigation by the FBI. When questioned about his director's value, Groves called him "absolutely essential to the project."

After the war, Oppenheimer was named chairman of the General Advisory Committee of the Atomic Energy Commission. Like many scientists at the time, he lobbied for international arms control. In 1953, the FBI accused him of being a security risk, and he was subjected to a lengthy hearing on his political views. As a result of the hearing, his security clearance was revoked. Many members of the scientific community saw him as a martyr who was unfairly attacked by paranoid conservatives with political power. Stripped of his political influence, Oppenheimer traveled the world as a lecturer.

had fallen on hard times in recent years and was eager to explore a buyout. In November, the U.S. government began to buy up pieces of the property. All in all, they paid $440,000 for the land and buildings, as well as 60 horses and assorted classroom materials. The home of the Manhattan Project officially opened on April 15, 1943.

U.S. TROOPS HIT THE GROUND

Meanwhile, the first American troops to engage in combat in the Western Theater landed in North Africa in November 1942 to join British forces. Unfortunately for the Allies, there was little organization among their ranks, and the American troops were not yet battle-experienced. On January 23, 1943, Montgomery's Eighth Army captured Tripoli and cut off Rommel from his main supply base. When the 5th Panzer Army encountered the Allies on January 30, the Allies were overrun and suffered many losses. Tunisia fell into German hands. With nowhere else to go, the U.S. 1st Armor Division retreated to the Kasserine Pass, which would be easier to defend. Because of poor tactics, they soon found themselves trapped. British and French troops came to their rescue, and the Allies were able to prevent the Germans from advancing. While the Panzer divisions easily defeated the Americans, they also spread themselves thin along a longer and longer battlefront. Fearing the battle line would be broken, Rommel retreated to form a strong defense. A U.S. air attack drove him out of the pass, which once again fell into the hands of the Americans.

By March 1943, the 8th Army had reached the Tunisian border, using the U.S. II Corps as a pincer to trap Rommel and his army. They squeezed the Axis forces, which surrendered on May 13, handing the Allies more than 275,000 prisoners of war. The loss of so many experienced soldiers was a big blow to the Axis powers.

NORTH TO ITALY

After driving the Germans and Italians out of Africa, the Allies set their sights on Italy. In July 1943, the Italian Campaign was launched with the Allied invasion of Sicily, an Italian-held island off the coast of mainland Italy. Allied forces proved to be too strong for the Italian soldiers. A string of defeats led the Italians to grow distrustful of Hitler. Italian leaders turned away from their loyalties to Mussolini and began to support the king, who eventually ordered Mussolini to resign. Pietro Badoglio succeeded Mussolini and immediately began negotiating surrender with the Allies in Italy. An armistice, or temporary suspension of hostilities, between the Allies and Italy was signed September 3, 1943. The Germans, however, knew the Italians would surrender and sent in forces to occupy the northern part of the country.

Mussolini, who had been arrested by the new government, was rescued by German special forces and was placed as head of a new German state in northern Italy called the Italian Social Republic. As the Allies continued to fight their way northward, Italians overthrew the Italian Social Republic on April 25, 1944. Mussolini was captured by these Italians and, along with his mistress, executed by machine gun and hung upside down from a street lamp. The Germans retained control of northern Italy until the end of the war, but by mid-1944, Italy was no longer a factor in deciding the outcome.

MERCHANT SHIPPING IN THE ATLANTIC

During the course of World War II, one of the most hotly contested areas was the Atlantic Ocean. From early on, the Allies knew the key to holding Britain was shipping. The British war machine required guns, planes, tanks, ships, and oil. The British people needed food and other raw materials to sustain industry. Britain produced only one-third of the food it required and relied on imports for the rest. Germany did its best to cut off the shipping lanes through which vessels carrying goods to Britain traveled. The Allies quickly realized that if they were going to win the war, they would have to control the Atlantic.

The Allies planned to support merchant ships with naval escorts and air support. There were two problems with this strategy. Battleships were in short supply, and planes did not have enough range to cover the Atlantic without having to turn back to their bases to refuel. Thus, a vast portion of the

In the early stages of World War II, German U-boats sunk many Allied ships in the Atlantic Ocean. In response to this threat, Allied forces dropped depth charges in an attempt to destroy these hidden vessels. *Above*, coast guardsmen on the cutter *Spencer* watch a depth charge explosion on April 17, 1943.

Atlantic was unprotected by airpower. In addition, the Germans had lethal submarines, called U-boats, that lay in wait for British ships. They could fire torpedoes and retreat into the depths, undetected.

During the early part of the war, the German U-boats were nearly unstoppable. British convoys, typically totaling 40–50 merchant ships and escorted by a few naval ships, were vulnerable. Large numbers of merchant ships were sunk by U-boats at a great cost of ships and the lives of those who sailed them. However, several technological developments during the course of the war made it difficult for the U-boats. One of those developments was sonar. The Allies used sonar to detect the noise made by the U-boats when they fired torpedoes. Sonar allowed them to estimate the location of a U-boat, at which point warships would drop underwater bombs, called depth charges, with the hopes of disabling the enemy submarines. Another development was the small aircraft carrier, a ship with a built-in airstrip from which planes could take off and on which they could land. Armed with their own small air forces, British ships could attack both U-boats and German ships from any location in the Atlantic.

As the war progressed, Britain and the United States supplied more naval ships to escort merchant shipping. Planes were built to hold more fuel, extending their range and enabling them to protect shipping convoys deeper into the Atlantic. By 1944, when the Allies planned an invasion of mainland Europe, the Allies had sunk most of the German U-boats and battleships, making the journey from America to Britain a relatively safe trip.

PREPARATIONS FOR THE BATTLE OF NORMANDY

By May 1944, the Allies had driven the Italians and Germans out of North Africa. Italy had no strategic importance. The beaches of England were secure. The vast majority of German troops were positioned on the eastern front, where they engaged the Russians in a long, brutal campaign. For the Allies, the next logical step was to send troops into mainland Europe to take back France. Because most of the German troops were fighting the Russians, only 400,000 Germans guarded France's Atlantic coast. In contrast, the Allies offered 120 divisions that totaled more than 2 million soldiers. Most were American, with about 600,000 British soldiers and a smaller number of Canadian, French, and Polish troops. Until this point in the war, most of the fighting in Europe had taken place between the Russians and the Germans on the eastern front. By sending masses of troops and equipment to western France, the Allies would create a second front. The hope was that the second front would draw German troops away from the battles with the Russians, spreading them thin and making them more vulnerable. It would also enable the Allies to squeeze the Germans from both the east and west.

Prior to the invasion, the Allies had heavily bombed German industry, crippling their enemy's capacity to replenish aircraft, ships, tanks, and small arms. In essence, the Germans would have to fight the remainder of the war with what they had. Still, Allied commanders realized the difficulty in overrunning a German army that had established effective defensive positions along the coast of France. So in the months preceding the invasion, the Allies began a campaign of deception to trick the Germans. They created a fake operation they hoped would convince the Germans they would first attack the Balkan Islands or the Pas de Calais. They also led the Germans to believe they would attack Norway so that the Germans would send troops there to defend their holdings. The Allies positioned double agents within the German ranks to feed false information. They also placed dummy tanks and landing craft along the ports of eastern Britain, which they did not protect with planes, enabling German pilots to photograph them. In addition, they sent radio broadcasts of static noise so that the Germans would spend their resources trying to decode white noise and distracting them from the actual invasion site. The night before the invasion, Allied planes dropped dummy paratroopers over Le Havre and Isigny, drawing the Germans to focus on those areas. That night, they also dropped a large number of tinfoil strips in the ocean 15 miles from Le Havre. The foil would show up on enemy radar and lead the Germans to believe a small convoy of ships was heading there.

U.S. general Dwight D. Eisenhower would command the operation. The troops would be supported by 6,900 ships and landing craft and 12,000 aircraft, mostly bombers. In the initial phase of Operation Overlord, the Allies would land at several beaches along the Normandy coastline and establish defensive positions. It was hoped they would secure the beaches and then bring in two artificial harbors, called Mulberry harbors, that would make it easier for supply ships to "dock" close to the beach, where they could quickly unload supplies for the invading forces. They also planned to install a series of underwater pipes to carry fuel from Britain to the invading forces.

Eisenhower had chosen the night of June 5 for the assault. Typically, the weather on the Normandy coast turned for the worse in June. It was often cloudy and foggy, and the seas grew rough. Because the brief window of favorable weather had closed, the Germans did not expect the Allies to attack. When June 5 arrived, the weather prohibited an attack. Allied commanders feared the weather would hold and further delay the operation, but the next day, the skies had cleared just enough to make an air attack feasible. On the morning of June 6, 1944, Operation Overlord began.

D-DAY

The day began with heavy airborne landings by the U.S. 82nd and 101st Airborne Divisions and the British 6th Airborne Division. Paratroopers jumped from planes to landing sites inland from the coast and attempted to secure areas toward which troops landing on the beaches would drive the Germans. The night before, battleships and troop carriers sailed from Britain across the English Channel over rough seas. Most of the soldiers suffered seasickness as they sailed through the night. As they neared the coast of France, the ships unleashed their big guns on the German artillery.

The ships fanned out over five beaches: Sword, Juno, Gold, Omaha, and Utah. Most Allied troops were quick to establish a solid defense and keep the Germans at bay. But the American forces landing on Omaha Beach hit a wall of German fury. Omaha Beach was the most heavily fortified of the five beaches, and German gun placements were well protected from Allied air strikes. The initial landings suffered heavy casualties. Almost every soldier was gunned down as soon as he disembarked the landing craft and ran onto the beach. Others were shot in the water or drowned under the weight of their heavy loads. More than 3,000 American troops were killed on Omaha Beach in the span of the first day of the invasion. Still, the carriers unloaded troops.

Finally, a small group of survivors, hiding behind the barbed wire and wooden obstacles placed by the Germans, established a small, secure area where tanks and armored vehicles were able to land. These vehicles helped in providing cover fire, and eventually the Allies were able to safely land a number of troops. These were able to assault the German gun placements and, after a long, bloody battle that saw many casualties on both sides, take control of the beach. Many of these gun placements were perched atop steep cliffs, and the only way to reach them was by climbing ropes.

By the day's end, more than 150,000 Allied troops had landed on the beaches. The initial stage of the operation was a success. From there, the Allies fought their way east toward central France. By August 6, they had reached the Seine River and were in a favorable position to retake France.

The invasion of Normandy is considered the best-planned military operation of World War II. Despite the large number of Allied casualties, the defeat was more costly to the Germans, who relinquished vital ground as they retreated toward Germany. The Soviets benefited from the landings as well, as large numbers of German troops were withdrawn from the eastern front in an effort to contain the invaders. German morale was virtually destroyed, as Axis commanders watched their armies confronted on two sides by strong Allied forces. To many, the success marked the end of the war for Germany. From that point on, it would be only a matter of time before the Allies overran Germany.

THE WESTERN FRONT

By August 1944, the Allied forces in Europe had spread out across France in attempt to establish a western battle line. The French Resistance, a group of armed French citizens who sabotaged Nazi occupation forces in Paris and in the surrounding countryside, rose up against German troops and aided in gaining the liberation of Paris on August 25, 1944. As Allied forces moved toward Germany, they encountered logistical problems that slowed their advance. They were still being supplied via Normandy, which meant that fuel and other necessities often arrived in a trickle. Aid came when the Canadian 1st Army cleared the entrance to the port of Antwerp, Netherlands, in November 1944 to help speed up the supply of Allied troops. Things were going well for the Allies. In October, Americans captured the city of Aachen. The Allies felt the war would be over before winter.

Hitler was not ready to give up his quest to rule Europe. He had been planning a major counteroffensive against the Allies. His sights were set on Antwerp, the Belgian port recently secured by the Allies. His intention was to disrupt the supply line to the Allies and thereby demoralize them to the point that

Allied leaders would be forced to negotiate. He sent his best forces through the Ardennes in southern Belgium, a heavily forested region where the Germans had been victorious in 1940.

THE BATTLE OF THE BULGE

Once the Allies had retaken France and crossed the German border, they were preoccupied with planning and preparing for offensive strikes. Hitler took advantage of this weakness as well as of the Allies overconfidence. He knew they believed they would end the war before winter, and he thought that their offensive-minded tactics would put them at a disadvantage should he attack. Plus, his armies were no longer defending Europe. They were more concentrated and closer to the German border, making resupply easier than it had been in the past. Now it was the Allied forces that were spread from France to the Netherlands. In total secrecy, he and the German command planned an attack on Antwerp.

His goal was to cut off the Allied supply lines and to divide the enemy army in half, attacking and encircling the American armies and forcing the Allies to negotiate a peace treaty in favor of the Axis powers. During the resulting lull in fighting, he believed the Germans would produce more advanced weapons such as jet planes and heavier tanks. In hindsight, Hitler's view could not have been less realistic. Although he believed American troops were poorly trained and had little resolve, in actuality they were the strongest and the most readily reinforced or replaced troops on the battlefield.

The surprise attack fell upon the U.S. 1st Army, which guarded the weakest section of the Allies' line. In fact, Allied intelligence considered the Ardennes a quiet spot and even used the area for the training of new troops. Thus, many of the soldiers in the immediate area were inexperienced in combat or battle-weary troops who were sent there to recover. If Hitler had been wrong about the overall strength of the American forces, he was right about this weak link.

Aerial warfare became an important factor in World War II, especially during the Battle of the Bulge. Desperate to strike back at the Allied forces, Hitler planned an attack in a weakly defended area of the Ardennes forest. While American ground forces were able to hold back the Nazis, U.S. aircraft shot through the skies and destroyed many of the enemy. Still, almost 80,000 American soldiers were killed, captured, or maimed during this battle, one of the bloodiest in U.S. history.

On December 16, 1944, the 6th SS Panzer Army let loose their artillery on Allied troops. By 8:30 A.M., all three German armies had attacked. The 5th Panzer Army, which attacked in the middle, killed at least 7,000 Americans. These forces advanced, pushing the middle of the battle line forward, creating a "bulge." It was not until the next day that Eisenhower realized the Ardennes was a major offensive. Within a week, 250,000 troops had been sent as reinforcements. Once the weather cleared, the Americans were aided by air strikes. While they were holding their newly won territory, the German forces were depleted. They turned to tactics of disruption, such as dressing soldiers in American uniforms and infiltrating them behind Allied lines. Many of these were captured and spread disinformation about German tactics. It was clear the Germans were desperate, yet they continued to fight strongly at the center of attack.

With the air assault, the Allies were able to stall the German advance and eventually drive the Germans to retreat. On January 7, 1945, Hitler ordered the withdrawal of German troops from the Ardennes.

The U.S. forces saw more troops killed in the Battle of the Bulge than in any other battle in World War II. They used more troops and fought against more Germans than in any other conflict. In the end, there were 19,000 American dead, with an estimated 80,000 total casualties. As for the Germans, they had exhausted the last of their reserve troops, and they never realized their objectives of cutting the Allied forces in half and negotiating a favorable peace treaty. Their depleted units retreated.

THE WAR IN EUROPE ENDS

The Battle of the Bulge marked the end for Germany. Hitler's troops had suffered more than 100,000 casualties, and they had lost at least 600 tanks and 1,600 planes. The factories that produced this equipment had been bombed out of production, so they had no way of building more. As the German army retreated from the west, they destroyed bridges to hamper the Allied advance. It took the Allies six weeks to reach Germany.

Meanwhile, the Russians were advancing from the east. German troops still put up a heavy resistance, but Stalin's troops were much stronger. As the Russians moved in, the Germans fought harder. Pushed back into the German capital of Berlin, they inflicted heavy casualties on their enemy. The fighting in Berlin involved tanks and even hand-to-hand combat. By then, Berlin was nearly a pile of rubble. During the battle, the Soviets suffered 360,000 casualties. The Germans sustained 450,000 casualties, with another 170,000 captured. As for Hitler, he and his staff remained holed up in a concrete bunker beneath the Chancellery. Sensing the end of his dream, on April 30, 1945, he committed suicide.

After Hitler's death, the German war effort was essentially finished. German troops surrendered to the Soviets on May 2, 1945. By May 7, German troops all over Europe surrendered, and the next day, May 8, 1945, the German surrender was signed and the Allies celebrated V-E Day. Meanwhile, the Manhattan Project moved forward at a lightning pace. Even though the Germans had been defeated, the bomb would be built.

V-E DAY

The fall of Berlin marked the end of the war in Europe. Just before midnight on May 8, 1945, delegates from the Soviet Union, the United States, France, and Great Britain met with representatives of the German command and signed the German Act of Unconditional Surrender.

For most of Europe, the war was finally over. The French, whose country had been overrun by Hitler's Nazis and who lived in fear during the period of German rule, at last could restore their own government. The British, who had fought back the Nazis and had seen much of the capital city of London severely bombed, could begin to rebuild. It was a time of joy and relief.

Huge celebrations broke out in London, where more than a million civilians greeted King George VI, Queen Elizabeth, and Prime Minister Winston Churchill at Buckingham Palace. Meanwhile, Americans took over the streets in big cities and small towns alike, including New York City, Chicago, and Los Angeles. President Truman celebrated in his own way, dedicating the victory to former president Franklin D. Roosevelt who had died the previous month. For the Europeans and Americans, the taste of victory was sweet.

5 The Pacific Theater

After the Japanese had successfully attacked Pearl Harbor in 1941, they set their sights on controlling the Pacific. Well prepared and fierce, the army and navy were unstoppable. Within just six months after the lightning raid on Pearl Harbor, the Japanese had occupied Malaya, the Philippines, Hong Kong, Singapore, and Burma. By controlling these territories, Japan was in a position to access resources necessary to fuel its war machine, such as oil and rubber, and to control the waters of the western Pacific.

MALAYA, SINGAPORE, AND THE PHILIPPINES

On December 8, 1941, almost immediately after the attack on Pearl Harbor, the Japanese attacked the British colony of Malaya. Because Japan had not been considered an immediate threat, the British were unprepared to defend Malaya. Most of the British troops were battling the Germans in the Middle East, and they had far fewer men and planes than the Japanese. The Japanese easily won the battle, sinking two British battleships in the process. Under siege, the British retreated to the island of Singapore, which lay at the southern tip of Malaya.

There were 80,000 troops and substantial ground artillery defending Singapore, but all of the big guns faced south toward the sea. After moving more troops to the area over a period of weeks, the Japanese attacked from the north and avoided the antiaircraft artillery. They bombed the island and then landed three divisions of soldiers. The Japanese proved to be too strong for the Allied soldiers, and on February 15, 1942, Singapore surrendered. At that stage, the Japanese controlled the strategically located port from which they could launch other attacks.

Meanwhile, Japan was already at work invading other strategically important islands. Only hours after the victory

Bataan Death March

Throughout the war, the Japanese were known for their brutal treatment of prisoners of war. No other incident speaks to the cruelty of the Japanese troops in World War II more than the Bataan Death March. The incident began on April 9, 1942, when Major General Edward King Jr. surrendered some 75,000 prisoners to the Japanese, who after a bloody battle had captured the Bataan peninsula in the Philippines. At the time of surrender, many of the Allied forces, consisting primarily of Filipinos, supplemented by nearly 12,000 American soldiers, were hungry and sick with tropical diseases.

The Japanese had planned to intern their prisoners in a camp more than 60 miles from Bataan. With no means to transport so many troops, they organized a rapid march to the camp. As far as the Japanese were concerned, the prisoners did not deserve to live. After all, these men had been captured at Pearl Harbor, Japanese troops had infiltrated numerous areas of the Philippines, a chain of islands just east of Malaya. They met little resistance and quickly ran the Americans out of the capital city of Manila. General Douglas MacArthur and his staff retreated, while General Edward King Jr. and 75,000 American and Filipino troops surrendered at the Battle of Bataan, the turning point of the fighting in the Philippines. Later, MacArthur uttered his famous words, "I shall return."

Japan then attacked the island of Formosa, which is now called Taiwan. There they destroyed more than 100 Allied airplanes, which allowed them to continue fighting without worry of American planes shooting from above. They also attacked the

and, thus, defeated. To their way of thinking, death was more honorable than defeat.

They took the prisoners' belongings and forced them, at gunpoint, to march. Along the way, the prisoners were denied food and water. If a prisoner stopped to rest or fell from exhaustion, he was severely beaten or killed. The same treatment was given to men who tried to assist fallen prisoners. Others were killed for sport, shot randomly or stabbed with bayonets. Many prisoners tried to escape into the jungle and were shot. Others escaped and found themselves lost in the dense, unfamiliar jungle, starving, wounded, and hunted.

Though it is impossible to pinpoint an exact figure, historians estimate some 10,000 prisoners died on the march. About 5,000 escaped into the jungle. When the war in the Pacific ended, Masaharu Homma, the Japanese commander who was responsible for ordering the march, was tried, convicted, and executed for his role in the atrocious war crime.

Dutch East Indies, which they captured in late February 1942. They moved on to take the island of Corregidor, which included a substantial American base. The Americans had been so devastated by the Japanese attacks that they were forced to surrender the base at Corregidor on May 7, 1942. Under the terms of the surrender, the United States officially surrendered the Philippines to Japan as well.

The Japanese quickly developed a reputation for their ruthless treatment of prisoners. As the United States, Britain, and Australia engaged in a grueling war in the Pacific, more and more Allied forces were captured. While the Nazis committed atrocities against the Jews, they treated non-Jewish prisoners of war largely in accordance with international law. But the Japanese were a different story. Japanese traditions of honor dictated they treat their prisoners with scorn and contempt. They forced prisoners to work in extreme conditions, often starving them and denying them medical attention. For example, they forced prisoners to build a railway in Thailand, literally working some 16,000 prisoners to death. Another example of their ruthless treatment of prisoners is the Bataan Death March. In 1942, when the Philippines fell to Japan, the Japanese forced thousands of U.S. and Filipino prisoners to march 60 miles to the camp where they would be interred. Suffering ungodly heat, a lack of food and water, and intense beatings by their captors, more than 10,000 prisoners died. The Allied propaganda machine used the ruthlessness of the Japanese to fuel support for the war in America, Britain, and France. As a result, citizens of Allied nations developed a strong hatred for the Japanese.

CORAL SEA

The Japanese army had plans to attack Australia, but first it had to establish a base nearby. It chose Port Moresby, a coastal town on what is now the island of Papua New Guinea, in the western Pacific Ocean. The United States had regrouped from the attack on Pearl Harbor. Because the Americans had broken the codes Japan used for radio communications, they were aware of Japan's intentions and had time to prepare for battle.

At the time, the Americans had three aircraft carriers in the western Pacific. They would be used to defend Port Moresby. The small American fleet had the assistance of the Australian fleet, which was positioned in the Coral Sea between Australia and Papua New Guinea. The Japanese were nearby but far enough away that they could not be seen. On May 4, 1942, both the Americans and Japanese sent out planes to scout the other's position. By May 7, the fighting had escalated; and by May 8,

Captured U.S. and Filipino soldiers were forced on the brutal Bataan Death March *(above)* to a Japanese POW camp 60 miles away. Already weak from a long battle, the prisoners were denied food and water and were treated savagely. When they reached the camp, Japanese treatment of the troops did not improve, and two out of three soldiers who were alive during the capture did not survive to the end of the war.

the Japanese had lost a light carrier, while the American fleet had lost the U.S.S. *Lexington*, a large carrier. There was no clear winner in the battle: The Japanese had won the battle of material by sinking the larger American ship, but the United States won the strategic battle by defending Port Moresby from a ground invasion. This was an important battle in the history of naval warfare in that it was the first battle at sea in which ships were sunk without ever having fired shots. Instead, the ships were sunk by fire from the air attack. In any case, the battle gave both navies experience that would be useful in the Battle of Midway, which occurred a month later.

THE BATTLE OF MIDWAY

Believing the U.S. Navy had been severely weakened, Japanese naval commanders organized the Battle of Midway to once and for all destroy their enemy's navy and to pressure the United States to admit defeat in the Pacific. Admiral Isoroku Yamamoto developed a complicated strategy that he planned to use to lure the American ships into a trap and sink them. He then planned to land troops on the atoll of Midway and take the American base. His intelligence showed there were only two functioning American carriers in the area: the U.S.S. *Enterprise* and the U.S.S. *Hornet*. The Japanese strike force consisted of four carriers and several, smaller support ships.

Admiral Yamamoto kept half of the fleet out of sight of the American ships and maintained radio silence so they would not be discovered. He sent the other half to Midway, where they would strike the Americans. The support ships would then join the battle, surprising the Americans with superior force and winning a victory. Unbeknownst to him, the Americans had broken the code the Japanese used to communicate over the radio, and they knew of the trap long before the plan was put into motion.

On the morning of June 4, 1942, as the Japanese strike force neared Midway, their scouting planes reported seeing 10

American ships. Yamamoto's supporting battleships and cruisers were still more than 100 miles away—too far away to engage in battle. American bombers had already taken off from the base at Midway and soon began to drop bombs on the Japanese ships. Likewise, Japanese planes bombed and shot at the American ships. Japanese antiaircraft guns destroyed all but three of the American bombers, which did almost no damage at all.

Both sides attacked and counterattacked by air and sea. Only one U.S. carrier was sunk: the U.S.S. *Yorktown*. In contrast, the Japanese lost four carriers and eight airplanes. By nightfall, both sides drew away, and the battle was over. The Americans had scored a decisive victory—their first in the Pacific.

The Battle of Midway marked a turning point in the war in the Pacific. Many historians consider it to be the most important naval engagement of World War II. It permanently weakened the Imperial Japanese Navy, which lost four carriers, a heavy cruiser, and more than 200 planes. At the time of the battle, the Americans were three years into an aggressive shipbuilding plan to grow the U.S. Navy to a size superior to Japan's navy. After the Battle of Midway, the United States was able to produce a steady stream of replacement ships, while Japanese ship production was at a standstill. Thus, for the first time, the Americans would be able to go on the offensive in the Pacific.

MOVING TOWARD JAPAN

For the next two-and-a-half years, the Americans, aided by the Australians, would battle the Japanese across the many islands that dot the Pacific from Papua New Guinea northward to Japan. Their first offensive occurred in August 1942 when U.S. Marines invaded Guadalcanal to destroy a Japanese airfield that was under construction. The resulting campaign was fierce and bloody. For six months, the Marines battled the Japanese in the humid jungle. In February 1943, Guadalcanal belonged to the United States.

As U.S. forces made their way from island to island, it became clear that they were better equipped to fight. While the Japanese were unable to replace the ships and airplanes lost in battle, the war machine in the United States was producing ships and planes at a high rate, and the American forces were able to quickly replenish their losses. The main reason Japan was unable to replace its ships and planes was the lack of resources needed to produce them. Whereas the Americans were rich in resources and had built highly effective production capabilities that would enable them to produce ships, planes, and tanks for a long time to come, the Japanese had no such capabilities. They had counted on a quick and decisive victory. The longer the war went on, the more likely their resources would be stretched to the breaking point.

Japan lacked the resources and production capabilities to produce combat vehicles, but it was also lacking another important resource: oil. American submarines, operating in the Pacific, played a major role in the defeat of Japan. They sunk Japan's merchant fleet, which carried oil and other valuable goods needed for weapons production. They also destroyed Japanese warships and troop transports. Submarines also provided intelligence on the location of the Japanese fleet, which was invaluable as the U.S. military command planned the island battles.

The Americans fought the Japanese but sometimes abandoned the islands on which they fought in order to move on to others. Gradually, they made their way closer to Japan. The generals were aiming to position American forces close enough to Japan to launch an all-out attack. In order to do this, they had to establish nearby air bases and secure the waterways so their battleships could shell the beaches of Japan prior to a ground attack. Throughout the course of the war in the Pacific, Japanese troops were competent and ruthless enemies. Many lives, both American and Japanese,

The Japanese planned the Battle of Midway *(above)* as a surprise offensive, but the U.S. military intercepted and deciphered their communications early enough to create a strong defense. The Japanese lost four of their best aircraft carriers, the same ones used in the attack on Pearl Harbor, while the United States lost only one.

were lost on those islands and atolls, and in the deep seas surrounding them.

THE PHILIPPINES REVISITED

In February 1942, when the Americans surrendered the Philippines to the Japanese, General Douglas MacArthur had vowed to return to the island to extract revenge. He knew that America could not win the war against Japan without first recapturing the Philippines. MacArthur's chance for redemption came nearly two years after the U.S. surrender. This time, the Americans were well prepared.

On October 20, 1944, the U.S. Sixth Army landed on the eastern shore of Leyte, while airplanes tore into the Japanese troops located on the western side of the island. After weeks of brutal fighting, the U.S. troops had secured their piece of the island and drove the Japanese away as they advanced north to the island of Samar. During the months of December and January, the United States continued to land troops on various islands of the Philippines. Pressure was exerted from the north and the south on the city of Manila. By April, the Philippines was largely secured.

After the Allies captured and secured the Philippines, Burma, and Borneo, the time had come to harass the Japanese on their own islands. Two islands in particular—Iwo Jima and Okinawa—held strategically important air bases the Americans wanted to capture and use for bombing raids of major Japanese cities, such as Tokyo. But capturing these islands would not be easy.

IWO JIMA

After the Allies had secured the Philippines, they had a two-month period of inactivity before the planned invasion of Okinawa. American commanders saw the opportunity to use troops already in the area to secure an air base on the island of Iwo Jima. This base had been used by the Japanese to launch planes that would intercept American B-29 bombers on their way to Japan. By capturing the air base, the Americans would eliminate the threat to their long-range bombers and have a new airstrip even closer to the best bombing targets in Japan. Army intelligence believed the island could be taken rather easily within a five-day period, but they had underestimated the resolve of the Japanese troops.

The Japanese were well prepared for the attack. In previous island engagements with the Allies, they had confronted enemy troops on the beaches, often sending wave after wave of soldiers out into the open to fight and die. This time, they took a different approach. Knowing that American warships would be bombarding the island with explosives and that planes would drop bombs to help soften the defense, the Japanese dug in. They built pillboxes (concrete-fortified structures) where they placed heavy machine guns and other large weapons. They also dug a complex system of tunnels and bunkers so that groups of troops could communicate with one another without having to risk exposure to enemy fire. The Japanese command expected defeat. Their main goal in the battle was to inflict heavy damage on Allied troops with the hope of discouraging them from attacking the main islands of Japan.

On the afternoon of February 19, 1945, battleships fired their guns on the island, and about 100 bombers attacked. Seven hours later, the first troops landed on the beach, taking fire from large Japanese guns on Mount Suribachi. The ground consisted of volcanic ash, which did not allow the Marines to dig holes for protection. Soon though, armored vehicles arrived to lead the troops from the beaches. By the end of the day, 30,000 Marines had landed. They would be reinforced by an additional 40,000.

The Allies worked to surround heavily fortified Mount Suribachi, which they hoped to capture before moving on to clean up the rest of Iwo Jima. By the fourth day of fighting, the Marines had surrounded the mountain, cutting it off from further supply. Scouts were sent up the mountain to determine the extent of enemy reinforcements. They returned to report they had met little resistance, so Colonel Chandler Johnson sent a platoon of Marines to the summit. The platoon was able to capture Mount Suribachi, where they hoisted the American flag.

After Mount Suribachi had been taken, the Marines moved on to capture the airfields and the rest of the island. Supported by heavy guns and armored vehicles that had been sent ashore recently, they moved north and inland. Over the next three weeks, the Marines faced a fierce enemy who was willing to fight to the death. They soon learned that their rifles and machine guns were not effective in killing the entrenched Japanese, so they began to use grenades and flamethrowers instead. Gradually, and with heavy losses, they were able to clear Japanese defensive positions and advance across the island. As the battle wore on, Japanese troops began making night raids on the Marines. These battles, often hand-to-hand, were disruptive yet otherwise ineffective.

By then the Japanese knew their situation was desperate. For them, honor was in death. To surrender to the enemy was disgraceful. As such, over the course of the 35-day battle, of the more than 21,000 Japanese soldiers who fought on Iwo Jima, 20,703 died, and 216 were captured. The Allies suffered their greatest losses in any battle, including the Battle of Normandy, with 6,825 dead and more than 19,000 wounded.

THE DECISION TO MOVE FORWARD

In the late winter of 1945, victory in Europe seemed inevitable. The U.S. Army had poured billions of dollars into the Manhattan Project to build a bomb that would put an end to Hitler's Germany. If the Third Reich was essentially defeated, did it make sense to proceed with the costly project? While military officials discussed the pros and cons, no one involved with the Manhattan Project even paused to consider the option of stopping, now that they were only months away from testing the device.

As for military officials, they reasoned that the defeat of Japan could end up costing an enormous number of American lives and that the atomic bomb could help them win the war without huge losses. But strategists also reasoned the Soviets

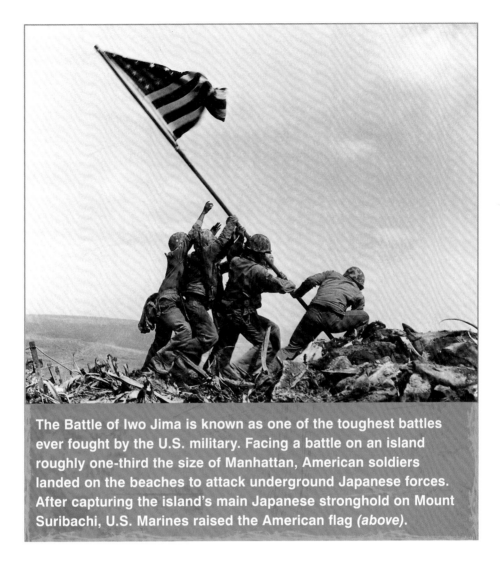

The Battle of Iwo Jima is known as one of the toughest battles ever fought by the U.S. military. Facing a battle on an island roughly one-third the size of Manhattan, American soldiers landed on the beaches to attack underground Japanese forces. After capturing the island's main Japanese stronghold on Mount Suribachi, U.S. Marines raised the American flag *(above)*.

were a bigger long-term concern. The Americans expected the Soviets would join them in battling Japan and in return expect a bigger piece of Europe or Asia in return, once the spoils of war were divided among the victors. By defeating Japan before the Soviets came to their aid, the Americans could control the postwar Soviet reach without messy diplomacy. For these immediate reasons, the Manhattan Project moved forward at full speed.

OKINAWA

The Allies had been planning an invasion of the Japanese island of Okinawa for some time. They wanted to seize the island and use it as a staging ground for operations that would involve an invasion of mainland Japan. If they were able to drive the Japanese out of Okinawa, they could use the air bases to launch B-29 bombers and even smaller fighter planes.

The Japanese command knew the attack was coming. Over the past three years, the persistent Allies had pushed them back across the islands of the western Pacific, and at last, their backs were against the proverbial wall. Taking note of the lessons they learned in the attempted defense of Iwo Jima, they chose the historical capital, Shuri Castle, as the center of their defense. The castle had been built as a medieval fortress at the edge of hills so steep that they could not be climbed.

Japanese general Mitsuru Ushijima knew that even if his troops put up a strong fight, the Allies were stronger. They had more troops in reserve that they could send in to relieve those fighting. They also had more planes, ships, and artillery. The Japanese had thousands of troops, as well as tanks and heavy guns. The artillery was placed in caves around the island. The artillerymen rolled the guns out to fire them, then rolled them back into the caves, where they were protected from enemy fire, to reload. But their strongest asset was their mastery of the terrain. They placed troops and guns in every cave they could find and placed others in positions advantageous to defending the island. Ushijima knew that the best he could hope for was to inflict heavy damages on the Allies and put a dent in their morale.

U.S. ground troops were supported by 1,300 ships, including 200 destroyers, 18 battleships, and 40 aircraft carriers. As the ships began to shell the island, Japanese planes, piloted by kamikazes, began to crash into the ships. Kamikaze pilots were trained to avoid antiaircraft fire and to pilot their planes straight into vulnerable parts of a ship. Naturally, these were suicide missions. When seamen spotted a Japanese plane diving toward them, they turned their guns on it and tried to blow it up before impact. In this particular campaign, kamikaze pilots were especially effective. In the 3-month battle, Japanese pilots flew 1,900 kamikaze missions, sinking dozens of ships and killing 5,000 sailors. The U.S. Navy sustained greater casualties in the invasion of Okinawa than in any other battle during World War II.

On April 1, 1945, Allied troops landed on multiple beaches on the western coast of Okinawa. Led by General Simon Buckner, the 10th Army quickly took control of the southern part of the island with little resistance. The rest of the battle would not be so easy. Over the next week, Allied forces fought battles all over the island, while planes dropped bombs and battleships shelled Japanese strongholds. The fighting was fierce, and both sides suffered enormous casualties.

At the beginning of June, the seasonal monsoon rains came and turned Okinawa into an island of mud. The constant, heavy rains and the deep mud made it difficult to walk or run. On both the battlefields and camps, dead Japanese were strewn about the ground. Over the weeks, the bodies decayed and became part of the muddy soup through which the soldiers lived and fought.

Finally, after nearly three months of constant fighting, the island fell. The United States lost 12,513 soldiers and had another 59,500 wounded—more than twice the number lost and wounded at the battles of Iwo Jima and Guadalcanal combined. Japanese losses were staggering. Some 66,000 Japanese troops were killed, and 7,000 were captured. Because the Japanese soldiers were trained to believe capture was far worse than death, many committed suicide rather than face the shame of defeat. In addition to the high number of military casualties, 140,000 civilians were killed or committed suicide as well.

Okinawa was won at a heavy price, but it was of such great strategic value that Allied commanders were willing to pay. The Allies gained airfields in close proximity to mainland Japan and a staging point for the long-planned ground invasion into the heartland of the enemy, an attack that would never come.

6 The Manhattan Project

Even before the brutal attack on Pearl Harbor and the declaration of war on the Axis powers, the United States had set its sights on building the first atom bomb. Most scientists and high-ranking members of the military agreed that such a destructive weapon could mean big trouble if it were to fall into enemy hands. As Germany built its army and made its intentions known, the development of nuclear weapons became a high priority for the U.S. government.

President Roosevelt had authorized research for the atomic bomb in 1939, at the urging of Alexander Sachs, Eugene Wigner, and Albert Einstein. But the project moved forward slowly for the first two years, as funding had to be secured and top physicists convinced to drop their own projects and sign on to work for the government. Roosevelt was also concerned, for several reasons, that the American public would resist such a project. For one, such work would require enormous fiscal resources. Another reason was that Americans as a whole wanted peace, not a weapon capable of destroying large numbers of people. Third, Americans knew about gunpowder, not physics. They were not familiar with the concepts surrounding atomic science. The whole idea of engineering a bomb powered by breaking apart something (an atom) that could not be seen by the naked eye was thought to be too abstract for most people to comprehend. In order to convince Congress and the American people to support such an endeavor, he needed a cause.

As plans were made to speed up the development of the bomb, that cause was delivered on a silver platter when the Japanese bombed Pearl Harbor. Once the United States entered the war, Roosevelt had all the support he needed to move forward. So in December 1941, the same month as the attack on Pearl Harbor, the U.S. government created a top secret plan to research and develop the atomic bomb. From that point on, the plan would be known as the Manhattan Project.

BREAKTHROUGH IN CHICAGO

The collection of scientists handpicked to participate in the Manhattan Project represented countries from all over Europe. Many were Jewish and had fled Hitler's persecution for the safety of the United States. They first gathered in Chicago, where they began the preliminary work that would lead to the world's first nuclear bomb. In fact, one of the first orders of business was to try to create a nuclear chain reaction, as Leo Szilard had proposed was possible some years earlier. A nuclear chain reaction occurs when the fission of a nucleus creates more nuclei that in turn automatically experience fission. It is important to note that these were all very "pie-in-the-sky" ideas at this point in history. Physicists were certainly aware of chemical chain reactions, but no one had ever conducted a nuclear chain reaction. Nonetheless, a handful of the world's top physicists gathered in Chicago to carry on with the work.

Within the year, the team had made great strides. In December 1942, beneath the bleachers of Stagg Field at the University of Chicago, Italian physicist Enrico Fermi built the world's first atomic pile. This device was a nuclear reactor in which the scientists triggered a controlled nuclear chain reaction. It was a great success in that it was the first nuclear chain reaction and because it confirmed that the physicists were on the right track with their theories.

Soon after, scientists from some 30 sites across the country gathered at a conference to discuss how to go about devising a plan to harness this chain reaction in the form of an explosive device. They discussed theories and potential paths to their end goal. The conference convinced J. Robert Oppenheimer, who headed the project, that the team would benefit from working together in a central location, rather than spread out across the country. Oppenheimer convinced the government

The Nuclear Chain Reaction

An atom bomb generates its massive explosive power by creating a nuclear chain reaction. This means that an initial nuclear reaction causes multiple other nuclear reactions, which in turn cause additional reactions, and so on.

An easy way to visualize this type of reaction is to think of tributaries branching off of a river. For example, say that the moment each tributary is created it sprouts three additional tributaries. The first tributary produces three additional tributaries. Each of those produce three more, and so on. It does not take long before you have a lot of tributaries. With each nuclear reaction in a chain reaction, energy in the form of heat and light is produced. As the reactions create more and more reactions, more and more energy is produced, resulting in extraordinary, explosive power.

that such a location was necessary not only to speed up the work but also to better maintain secrecy.

NEW PROJECT SITES

While two sites—one in Oak Ridge, Tennessee, and the other in Hanford, Washington—were created to generate the uranium needed to carry out the experiments, Oppenheimer looked to a familiar place for the main site. He proposed the site in Los Alamos, New Mexico, that he had known as a boy. The location became the "think tank" for the project and the place where the bomb would be constructed and tested.

These facilities were top secret, and it was only after the end of the war that the states in which they were located became aware of their size. The installation at Oak Ridge occupied a 93-square-mile plot of land and employed more than 82,000 people, making it the fifth-largest city in Tennessee. It consumed one-sixth of the electrical power produced in the entire United States, most of which was used to produce uranium. The motor transportation system was the largest in the southeastern United States, and there were more than 3,000 family quarters. The facility housed an entire school system, post offices, movie theaters, athletic fields, and even a newspaper. Yet no one outside of the upper echelons of government knew of it. The facility produced all of the materials necessary to carry out experiments in Los Alamos.

In turn, Los Alamos was a large undertaking. It housed 6,000 people, including scientists, technicians, and their families. The work was of such secrecy that most people who lived there were not permitted to know what others were working on. Code names were used for all references to materials, processes, and locations.

THE ARMY TAKES CHARGE

In early 1942, progress with the construction of the new sites lagged. The Office of Scientific Research and Development oversaw the entire project. Vannevar Bush, who had placed Army Chief of Staff George Marshall in charge, headed the office. Bush felt they could move the project along faster, so the army went in search of a man to head the project logistics.

Because of its remote location, an area of the Appalachian Mountains in Tennessee was an ideal spot for one of the Manhattan Project's three main sites. Oak Ridge eventually grew to be the fifth-largest city in the state. *Above*, a billboard at the Oak Ridge Facility in Tennessee warns workers and those involved in the Manhattan Project to stay quiet about their activities.

They chose Leslie Groves, who at the time had just finished overseeing the construction of the Pentagon, in Washington, D.C. Groves was known as a straight-forward, no-nonsense leader who got things done in a hurry. Anyone who doubted his methods or his will to get results was likely to be trampled.

Groves, who had hoped to be stationed overseas, accepted the project and threw himself into it headfirst. One of his first decisions was met with surprise. He appointed J. Robert Oppenheimer as the project's scientific director. Many were concerned that Oppenheimer's radical political views would pose security problems. But Groves recognized the scientist as a brilliant organizer who could understand just about anything and coordinate scientists and technicians to complete the complex mission. Over the next few years, Groves's choice of Oppenheimer as scientific director would prove to be a good one. Oppenheimer would be remembered as a man who had mastery of every scientific aspect of the project and as a diplomat who was adept at resolving conflicts between scientists and the military.

THE RACE FOR THE BOMB

While the Americans were getting the Manhattan Project up and running, the Germans were hard at work on their own quest to develop the nuclear bomb. Headed by renowned nuclear physicist Werner Heisenberg, the Germans took a different approach to the problem. While the American effort was built around uranium as the active ingredient, Heisenberg believed a material called heavy water (water with a high concentration of deuterium oxide) was necessary to create a nuclear reaction.

Allied efforts to prevent Germany from obtaining heavy water were largely successful, and when German resources grew scarce toward the end of the war, the project stalled before the scientists could reach their goal. However, the Allies were unaware that the Germans were not pushing ahead with the bomb, and they were motivated to reach their results in as short a time as possible because they feared the Germans would develop the bomb first. It is said that the scientists at Los Alamos crammed 30 years of work into a four-year period so they could beat the Germans to the punch.

THE FIRST ATOMIC EXPLOSION

Early in 1945, the scientists at Los Alamos were confident they could make a bomb that would utilize a nuclear chain reaction. They believed they could cause this reaction by using either the element uranium or plutonium. General Groves informed President Roosevelt that the first bomb would be ready for testing that summer. Two types of bombs were developed for the test. One used uranium; the other, plutonium. The uranium-based bomb was nicknamed "Little Boy." It worked like a gun, firing a single piece of uranium-235 into another. The second bomb, named "Fat Man," was more complex. It used conventional explosives to detonate a supply of plutonium-239. A test site was developed at the Alamogordo U.S. Army Air Base, in the desert of New Mexico. Oppenheimer named the test "Trinity" and later said the name came from one of poet John Donne's sonnets.

When President Roosevelt died in office in April 1945, Vice President Harry S. Truman became president. Up to this point, Truman had no knowledge of the Manhattan Project or even of the Allies' plan to develop a nuclear bomb. He was told about the top secret plans to develop nuclear weapons, and he was advised that a mass invasion of Japan to end the war would cost 500,000 American lives. Truman agreed the bomb would be the most effective solution to end the war. Immediately, his administration began to select possible Japanese sites favorable to such a bomb. Truman believed the bomb would help him to end the war quickly, to keep the Soviet Union from taking over Asia at the end of the war, and to test the new technology the United States had poured so much money into.

On July 16, 1945, the Trinity test was under way. Fat Man was rigged to a tower, suspended above the desert floor. Four hundred and twenty-five observers, including the key scientists and high-ranking army personnel, huddled in concrete bunkers. The closest bunkers were about six miles from the blast site. Even after years of development, no one knew if the bomb would work. There was great anticipation in the air as the final seconds ticked down. What the observers saw when the bomb detonated shocked them to the core. Although they wore sunglasses to protect their eyes from the anticipated bright light, they were unprepared for the blinding, multicolored energy that lit up the night sky. A growing roar followed. It knocked some observers to the floor, even though they stood behind thick concrete walls. The mushroom cloud rose 40,000 feet above the desert. The explosion had been even more powerful than the scientists had hoped. Its blast was equal to that of 18,000 tons of TNT. At the center of the explosion, which is referred to as ground zero, the temperature was three times hotter than the Sun's core.

It was reported that Oppenheimer turned to the man next to him and uttered a quote from the ancient Hindu text Bhagavad Gita: "Now I am become Death, the destroyer of worlds." (Oppenheimer mistranslated. The actual text reads, "Now I am become Time, the destroyer of all.") Later, he reflected that "We all knew the world would not be the same." Some rejoiced; others cried. Most were silent, stunned by the awesome destructive power of the device.

THE ACE UP THE SLEEVE

By May 1945, Germany and Italy had surrendered. All that remained was to defeat Japan, a task that seemed certain. The Japanese air force and navy had been destroyed. The United

States was in the middle of a heavy bombing campaign on Japan's major cities, creating great destruction. As the Allies prepared to send ground troops into Japan, the Japanese refused to meet the Allies' demand of unconditional surrender. Although some Japanese military leaders were in favor of ending the war, the majority insisted Japan preserve its honor by fighting to the end.

At the time of the Trinity test—July 1945—President Truman was at Potsdam, Germany. The Allied leaders—Truman, Winston Churchill, and Joseph Stalin—had set up a crucial meeting on the outskirts of Berlin to discuss the reorganization of Europe and the progress of the war with Japan. This was a critical time for American strategists. Not only did they want to end the war with Japan as soon as possible, they also wanted to keep Stalin from taking over Poland and other eastern European countries. The Soviets would surely reap significant spoils of the war, and they were strong enough to be a world power beside Great Britain and the emergent United Sates. Thus, they were a threat. In the short term, Truman wanted to convince Stalin to declare war on Japan. This, he thought, would certainly shorten the war.

Truman arrived in Germany with the knowledge that the atomic bomb was undergoing testing in New Mexico, and he anxiously awaited the results. A coded message arrived, indicating that the test had been a success. The president wrote in his diary, "We have discovered the most terrible bomb in the history of the world." Those around him, including Churchill, noticed a change. Where he had been rather tense going into the conference, once he had heard of the success at Trinity, he was ever more confident and relaxed. As far as he knew, the Manhattan Project had been carried out in total secrecy. The atomic bomb was now an ace he had up his sleeve. If Stalin were to make excessive demands in regard to the new world order, he could pull it out and stand up to the Soviet leader. In fact, he hoped to shock Stalin with the news.

Known as the "Journey of Death," the test area for the detonation of the world's first atomic bomb was equipped with three observation bunkers for scientists. When the bomb went off, a scientist standing five miles away was knocked over. The brilliant light of the explosion briefly blinded another scientist. Afterwards, the team discovered the test had incinerated the tower that held the bomb and turned the asphalt under it into green sand. The scientists knew from the results that the war was effectively over.

To Truman's surprise, when he told Stalin of the new weapon with never-before-seen destructive force, the Russian premier showed no reaction except to say that he hoped it would be put to good use against the Japanese. In fact, Stalin had known about the bomb all along. Unbeknownst to the Americans, he had placed Soviet spies inside of Los Alamos who informed him of the progress of the bomb's development. Nonetheless, Truman left the Potsdam Conference with what he wanted. The Soviets would declare war on Japan on August 15, within one month's time. More important, the resulting Potsdam Declaration served as one final warning to Japan to surrender or suffer total destruction.

THE DECISION TO DROP THE BOMB

While the leaders of Japan debated their country's future, the Americans listened in. They had cracked the Japanese codes and were able to intercept all of Japan's communications. They knew the minister of war, General Korechika Anami, wished to fight to the end and that others such as Japanese foreign minister Shigenori Togo and Emperor Hirohito favored peace. Hirohito wanted to use the Soviet Union as a moderator in negotiations with the other Allies. He had even planned to send representatives to Moscow to begin discussions on a peace agreement. But Japan's military leaders were uncompromising in their position that surrender was not an

The Potsdam Declaration and Hirohito: *A Sticking Point*

It is important to note that by this time of the war, the American people despised the Japanese. These feelings were due in part to the horrible ways in which Japanese soldiers treated their prisoners of war. But Americans were also subject to a government campaign of propaganda that painted all Japanese people as brutal and terrible. They felt Japanese emperor Hirohito was responsible for dragging them into the war. As a result, the American people wanted a total surrender.

At the same time, American politicians and military leaders were well aware that a total surrender would be tricky. They knew the Japanese people regarded Emperor Hirohito as a sacred figure who was as much a religious leader as he was a political figure. So the Allies were vague about the future of the emperor.

option, and many of the country's government officials feared they would be executed if they showed signs of meeting the Allies' demands.

On July 28, 1945, Japanese prime minister Suzuki rejected the terms of the Potsdam Declaration. He made a public announcement stating that Japan would continue to fight. This came as no surprise to the Allies. In fact, early in the summer of 1945, components of the atom bombs had been shipped in secret to Tinian Island in the central Pacific. Truman, it was later learned, had authorized the use of atomic bombs against Japan on July 25, 1945. Truman and his military leadership knew that many thousands of Japanese civilians would die as a result of an atomic bombing. After considering how the American people would accept such horrors, they concluded that such casualties were justified. After all, the Japanese had attacked Pearl Harbor unprovoked. They had also murdered and raped thousands of Chinese civilians and had subjected prisoners of war to horrific torture, labor, and long marches. A large number of Japanese civilian casualties was the price of victory, and Truman was ready to pay.

WAS THE ATOMIC BOMB NECESSARY?

Since the bombings, some historians have proposed that Japan would have surrendered to the United States even without the atomic bombs. Strategists claim that more conventional tactics, such as naval blockades combined with conventional bombing, would have done the job even without an invasion. They believe Truman's need to keep Stalin from claiming Poland and eastern Europe as the primary reason the atomic bombs were dropped. While most historians agree that this was significant motivation for Truman, not all believe the main reason he authorized the bombings was to defeat the Japanese. In an interview with *Sojourners Magazine*, noted historian Gar Alperovitz said:

The use of the atomic bomb, most experts now believe, was totally unnecessary. Even people who support the decision for various reasons acknowledge that almost certainly the Japanese would have surrendered before the initial invasion planned for November. The U.S. Strategic Bombing Survey stated that officially in 1946.

We found a top-secret War Department study that said when the Russians came in, which was August 8, the war would have ended anyway. The invasion of Honshu, the main island, was not scheduled to take place until the spring of 1946. Almost all the U.S. military leaders are on record saying there were options for ending the war without an invasion. . . .

Many scholars now believe that the president understood the war could be ended long before the November landing. J. Samuel Walker, a conservative, official government historian, states in his expert study . . . that the consensus of the scholarly studies is that the bomb was known *at the time* to be unnecessary.

After the war, Secretary of War Henry L. Stimson acknowledged that the Allies' strategy was "maximum force with maximum speed." He said, "No effort was made and none seriously considered to achieve surrender merely in order not to have to use the bomb." It was agreed that a show of massive force would bring Japan to an early surrender without the massive loss of American lives that would have come from an invasion.

7 Dropping the Bombs

By early August 1944, the Allies, led largely by U.S. forces, had captured most of the Pacific islands of strategic benefit between Hawaii and Japan. The goal was to establish a secure air base on an island within the B-29 bomber's range in the Mariana Islands of Guam, Saipan, and Tinian. The Allies had succeeded by winning a number of bloody battles on selected islands and establishing blockades around other Japanese strongholds, effectively cutting off their supplies.

Meanwhile, strategists went to work drawing up a list of potential targets for a nuclear attack. They wanted to choose a city that had not suffered notable damage from previous attack so that they could clearly show the devastating power of the bomb. The cities of Kyoto and Hiroshima were at the top of the list. But because Kyoto had great historical value as an ancient city, they chose the industrial complex of Hiroshima as a primary target.

In July 1945, General Groves and his team were busy on the island of Tinian assembling two atomic bombs, with plans to build more. The first, christened Little Boy, used a uranium core. The second, named Fat Man, used a plutonium core. By using two different bomb designs, the scientists could determine which was the most effective. As final preparations were made for the first attack, Little Boy was carefully loaded onto a specially configured B-29 bomber named *Enola Gay*, after commander Paul Tibbets's mother. Tibbets would be the pilot of the plane that dropped the first atomic bomb. Late on the night of August 5, the bomb had been loaded, and everything was in place for the mission.

IN FLIGHT

At 2:45 A.M. on August 6, 1945, *Enola Gay* took off from the airstrip on the island of Tinian. Two additional planes accompanied it, and weather planes flew ahead of the group. Aside from Colonel Tibbets, none of the crew knew what the plane carried or what the mission entailed. Officials and crew in the know had no idea if the crew would survive or if the plane would be engulfed in the blast. They kept their fingers crossed. As the *Enola Gay* neared Japan, the crew learned of its destination: "Hiroshima."

At 8:15 A.M., once over the Japanese city, Little Boy was dropped by parachute, and two of its three detonators were activated. The target was the Aioi Bridge, which lay at the center of the city. At 8:16, when the bomb was 1,903 feet above the ground, the crew activated the third and final detonator. The bomb exploded over the city, immediately killing 70,000 people in a blinding flash of heat and vaporizing most of the city. From the *Enola Gay*, tail gunner Sergeant George Caron recorded what he saw. He described a cloud of fire and a fast-rising column of smoke. On the ground, countless fires broke out, making the city look like a bed of coals. Then, the mushroom cloud, with a center of shooting flames, rose and spread out to a width of more than two miles. Thankfully for the crew, the plane was safely outside of its reach. Pilot Colonel Tibbets described the moments immediately following the blast as well: "A bright light filled the plane. The first

Chosen for its industrial and military value, Hiroshima was an ideal drop location for the first atomic bomb. After Little Boy was loaded into the B-29 bomber known as the *Enola Gay*, the crew set off for the Japanese city. The bomb was detonated directly above Hiroshima and created a large, mushroom-shaped cloud above the city *(above)*.

shock wave hit us. We were eleven and a half slant miles from the atomic explosion, but the whole airplane cracked and crinkled from the blast."

In the city, the initial flash incinerated thousands of people. An extremely hot wave of air extended from the epicenter, or the center of the explosion, killing people within a two-mile radius. Their flesh caught fire or their organs boiled. The heat wave was followed by an enormous shock wave that leveled buildings and sent large, scalding-hot pieces of iron and concrete in all directions. Choking clouds of dust and debris swirled through the city. As firestorms grew in intensity, a black, oily rain fell. All over the city, people died horrendously painful deaths. Those who had not already been killed by their bad burns tried to save themselves by jumping in the river. Most drowned. Those who made it would soon die of radiation poisoning.

After circling the city several times, the crew of the *Enola Gay* flew home in shock. While some of the crew expressed relief that the bomb worked and the mission was a success, others took a more broad perspective. Copilot Robert Lewis, who had verbally expressed such sentiments, wrote in a journal during the flight home, "My God, what have we done?"

A CITY IN RUINS

As the *Enola Gay* neared Tinian, Hiroshima burned. All radio, television, and telegraph facilities were inoperable. In effect, communications within the city were cut off. Emergency medical teams scrambled to set up makeshift hospitals, but there was little they could do to help. About 60,000 buildings had been destroyed, and tens of thousands of people were left homeless. Survivors fled to nearby villages, where they found overcrowding and food shortages. Within the next two weeks, even those who appeared to be uninjured would suddenly take ill and die of radiation sickness.

There are many accounts given by survivors of the blast at Hiroshima. All of them paint the same picture of horror and gore. Toshiko Saeki, who was 26 at the time, was at her parents' house in Yasufuruichi, just outside of Hiroshima, the day of the attack.

> Those of us who could move around were not treated [sic] the injured, but we were carrying dead bodies out of the building. I couldn't identify people by their faces. Trying to find my family, I had to take a look at their clothing, the clothes of the people who were still in the building. I couldn't find any of my family, so I went out to the playground. There were four piles of bodies and I stood in front of them. I just didn't know what to do. How could I find the bodies of my beloved ones. When I was going through the classrooms, I could take a look at each person, but these were mounds. If I tried to find my beloved ones, I would have to remove the bodies one by one. It just wasn't possible.

Yosaku Mikami, a 32-year-old fireman was on his way home from a 24-hour shift when the bomb exploded. He immediately went back to work.

> Since our order was to help the most heavily injured, we searched for them. We tried to open the eyes of the injured and we found out they were still alive. We tried to carry them by their arms and legs and to place them onto the fire truck. But this was difficult because their skin was peeled off as we tried to move them. They were all heavily burned. But they never complained but they felt pain even when their skin was peeling off.

Hiroshi Sawachika, a 28-year-old army doctor, described walking into a room full of people who sought medical treatment hours after the blast.

When I stepped inside, I found the room filled with the smell that was quite similar to the smell of dried squid when it has been grilled. The smell was quite strong. It's a sad reality that the smell human beings produce when they are burned is the same as that of the dried squid when it is grilled. The squid—we like so much to eat. It was a strange feeling, a feeling that I had never had before. I can still remember that smell quite clearly.

Finally, Akihiro Takahashi, who was 14, was at his school that day. He described his journey toward the Ota River, where he went to seek relief from his bad burns and peeling skin.

The bomb's blast sent out shock waves that leveled Hiroshima. Shards of glass from broken windows flew through the air as buildings crumbled and collapsed throughout the city. Fewer than 10 percent of the buildings in the city remained standing, and 9 out of 10 people living within a half-mile of the drop site died minutes after detonation.

We walked toward the river. And on the way we saw many victims. I saw a man whose skin was completely peeled off the upper half of his body and a woman whose eye balls were sticking out. Her whole body was bleeding. A mother and her baby were lying with a skin completely peeled off. We desperately made a way crawling. And finally we reached the river bank. At the same moment, a fire broke out. If we had been slower by even one second, we would have been killed by the fire. Fire was blowing into the sky becoming 12 or even 15 feet high.

News of the attack reached Japanese officials almost immediately, but they assumed Hiroshima had been the target of a severe conventional bombing raid. Attempts to reach the Army Control Station in Hiroshima were futile. Considering that radar had shown only a few planes in the vicinity, the Japanese were puzzled by the total silence of Hiroshima. Tokyo's first knowledge of the extent of the damage came from a statement issued by the White House some 16 hours following the attack.

TRUMAN AND JAPAN RESPOND

On August 6, 1945, President Truman issued public statements threatening the Japanese with total annihilation if they did not accept his terms of surrender. He said, "If they do not accept our terms, they may expect a rain of ruin from the air the like of which has never been seen on this earth." In Los Alamos, the scientists were overjoyed that their years of hard, secretive work had paid off. U.S. soldiers were thrilled and relieved that they would soon be going home.

But the Japanese refused to surrender. They did not release a public statement until August 8, two days after the attack on Hiroshima. A broadcast over Radio Tokyo described the grim scene in Hiroshima and made the statement that by dropping the atomic bomb the United States had made an enemy "for ages to come."

NAGASAKI

On the morning of August 9, three days after Hiroshima, Fat Man was loaded onto the B-29 bomber named *Bock's Car.* Although the primary target was the city of Kokura, the actual target remained undetermined and dependent on weather. Major Charles Sweeney piloted the plane, which, like *Enola Gay,* was escorted by support craft. When *Bock's Car* approached Kokura, the crew was unable to visually confirm the target, a criterion that was necessary for the bomb to be deployed. The plane circled, but the cloud cover would not break. Low on fuel, Sweeney was faced with a difficult decision. He could drop the bomb into the ocean without detonating it, or his crew could to try to hit the shipbuilding city of Nagasaki. He turned the plane toward Nagasaki, but when they arrived, they found a thick cloud cover that prohibited them from seeing the target. Just as the flight crew was about to give up, the clouds parted. At 11:01 A.M., they got a visual on the city and let the bomb go.

Fat Man, though more powerful than Little Boy, had less devastating effects. The city of Nagasaki was surrounded by hills that lessened the bomb's impact. About 50 seconds after the bomb was dropped, it reached an altitude of 1,540 feet and was detonated. The actual epicenter of the blast was two miles from the planned target. Still, about 70,000 of the city's 240,000 people died instantly. Others received lethal doses of radiation that would lead to sickness and death within weeks. About one-third of the city was leveled by the resulting blast.

Although the effects of Fat Man were not as devastating as those of Little Boy, it served to demonstrate the aim of the United States to bring Japan to surrender at any cost. Japanese military leaders, still in shock from the bombing of Hiroshima, still refused to surrender.

SURRENDER AT LAST

By now Japan was in great peril. The Americans were destroying the country by never-before-seen means, and the Soviets

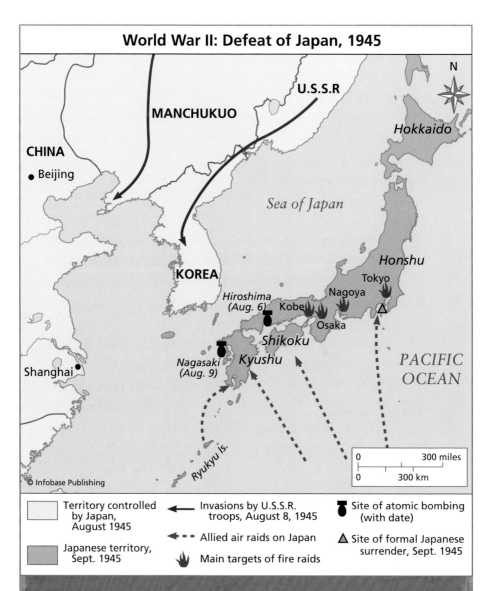

After virtually destroying Hiroshima, President Truman called on Japan to surrender. With Hiroshima destroyed in southern Japan, fire raids in northern Japan, and Russian forces invading other Asian territories, the Japanese boldly refused to give up. Truman then authorized the use of the second bomb on Nagasaki. This map shows the military strategy used to defeat Japan.

had officially declared war on them. The Japanese leaders had steadfastly remained resistant to the Allies' demands for surrender. But the time had come to reconsider these demands, and on August 9, 1945, Emperor Hirohito authorized Minister of Foreign Affairs Shigenori Togo to tell the Allies that Japan would accept the terms so long as he, Hirohito, could remain ruler of Japan.

Truman and his staff carefully considered this option and offered a reasonable compromise. They would allow Hirohito to remain on the throne so long as he was subject to the command of the Allied powers. They also promised that in the future Japan would be permitted to choose its own form of government. As the Japanese debated the new terms, the United States considered its own options. A third atomic bomb was ready for deployment, but Truman ordered a halt to the dropping of atomic bombs. He felt the Japanese were close to surrender, and he was troubled by the idea of destroying another city and killing tens of thousands more innocent Japanese civilians. So he ordered an intense campaign of conventional bombs on Japanese cities to further pressure Hirohito.

Then, on August 14, Hirohito's announcement of surrender was broadcast to the Japanese people. In his statement, he stressed that an enemy with such a powerfully destructive weapon could obliterate the entire nation of Japan forever as well as lead the human race into extinction. Most Japanese people had never before heard the godlike emperor's voice, and although they may not have understood his high-minded language, one thing was clear—the war was over. On September 2, 1945, Japanese military officials boarded the U.S.S. *Missouri*, a battleship positioned off of Japan, where they signed an official surrender. At last, the Allies had defeated Japan.

8 The Legacy of World War II

Immediately following the surrender of Japan, U.S. forces, led by General Douglas MacArthur, occupied the country. Although some of Japan's most militaristic officials were tried and hanged for war crimes, the rebuilding of the country started soon after the occupation began. But thousands of Japanese civilians from Hiroshima and Nagasaki were now showing advanced signs of radiation sickness. Their hair and teeth had fallen out. Painful sores opened on their flesh. They suffered severe diarrhea and fever. Most women who were pregnant at the time of the bombings had miscarriages. Many people died. Others lived with the sickness. Those who survived were given no special care or financial aid to help resume their lives. The Allies censored the Japanese press from reporting on the bombings or their aftermath. People were forbidden to come forward with their accounts.

These survivors are called *hibakusha*, which means "explosion-affected people." There are approximately 251,800 *hibakusha* recognized by the Japanese government today. Memorials constructed in Hiroshima and Nagasaki list the names of nearly 400,000 *hibakusha* who have died since the bombings, though not all have died because of the bombings.

The Cities of Hiroshima and Nagasaki

Hiroshima lies on the coast of the Seto Inland Sea. The city is located on the broad, flat delta of the Ota River, which has seven channel outlets dividing the city into six islands that project into Hiroshima Bay. The city is almost entirely flat and barely above sea level. On one side is the sea. On the other side are the Chugoku Mountains. Hiroshima was founded in 1589 by Mori Motonari, a prominent feudal ruler in the sixteenth century. It became a major urban center during the Meiji period (1868–1912), when large numbers of people living in rural areas moved to the city. Later, it became a major industrial center, with a number of cotton mills and, later, weapons plants. During World War II, Hiroshima was home to Toyo Cork Kogyo Co, the automobile company that is now called Mazda. During the war, the company manufactured rifles and other weapons for the Japanese military.

Nagasaki is an old city. It was founded some time before 1500. It was the center of European influence in Japan from first contact with European explorers in 1542. At that time, a Portuguese ship landed there, and soon the area was settled by Europeans. The city itself lies at the head of a long bay that forms the harbor of Kyushu. Two rivers divided by a mountain run toward the harbor. Its geography made it a suitable place for trade, and the village grew into a port where a wide variety of goods were traded. Throughout the next three centuries, Nagasaki remained a city whose economy was based largely on foreign trade. During the later part of the nineteenth century, the city became known as the center of shipbuilding in Japan and achieved economic dominance.

These memorials serve as a reminder to all Japanese, and to the world, of the horrors of nuclear war.

THE LEGACY OF THE BOMB

One of the most significant and lasting effects of World War II is the atomic bomb. Never before has a military weapon had such an impact on the psyche of the world's population. As countries such as Britain, China, France, and the Soviet Union acquired nuclear bombs, the division between the Western democracies and the Communist Bloc countries, led by the Soviet Union, became ever more profound. Both sides armed themselves to the hilt, first with nuclear bombs, then with the more powerful thermonuclear hydrogen bombs, and eventually with intercontinental missiles that could deliver nuclear warheads from one continent to another with the push of a button. They then used the threat of deployment as a deterrent to undesirable political action.

The period from the mid-1940s through the early 1990s was known as the Cold War. It was a war, not of battlefield fighting, but of espionage and political posturing. In a time of great tension, the United States and the Soviet Union embarked on a massive arms race, building their respective nuclear arsenals to the point that they could destroy all of civilization many times over. Although the countries never engaged in battle, several events, including the Cuban Missile Crisis (1962), brought the nations to the brink of nuclear war.

Countries with a world presence, such as the United States, still have as their most pressing concern the worldwide management of nuclear arms. Today, countries with unstable political parties or that are ruled by dictators pose the greatest threat. The United States and other countries continue to spend considerable resources to prevent these countries from acquiring the capacity to build and deploy nuclear weapons. What Truman once described as the greatest scientific gamble in history became an unprecedented legacy of military weaponry.

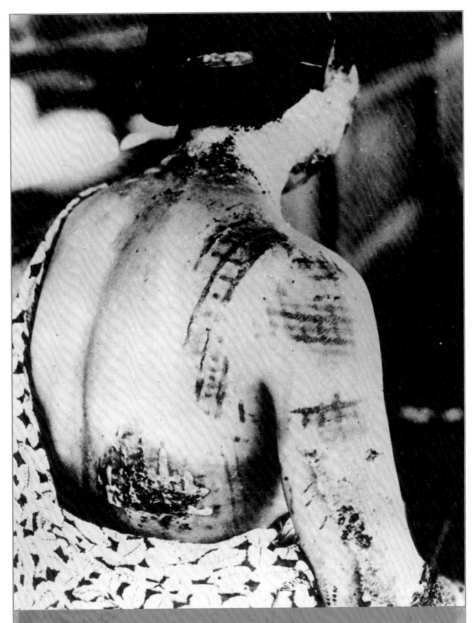

The intense heat and bright light that flashed through Hiroshima charred and blackened everything in its path, including people. Those who were farther away from the center of the blast were spared incineration, but they suffered terrible burns. *Above,* the flash burned the pattern of this woman's kimono into her skin.

A NEW WORLD ORDER

For many historians, World War II was the central event of the twentieth century and one of the most important episodes of modern history. In essence, it was an epic struggle of opposing ideologies played out in the skies, seas, and battlefields across the globe. In Europe, it pitted countries that enjoyed the spoils of World War I against countries whose leaders felt they had been shortchanged by the treaties that came out of that conflict and were determined to settle the score. While the war stopped the march of fascist dictators and their policies of enslavement and genocide, the restoration of global stability came at a great cost.

The United States armed forces alone saw 400,000 troops killed and a half-million wounded. Other nations suffered even greater losses. More than two million Japanese soldiers, pilots, and sailors were killed in battle. Between 20 and 30 million Russians died. All told, more than 25 million members of the military on both sides and 40 million civilians were killed. The estimated total loss of lives is 72 million human beings, making World War II the deadliest conflict in history.

After the war, many of the leaders and other influential figures of the Axis were held accountable for their actions during the war. The International Military Tribunal for the Far East, otherwise known as the Tokyo War Crimes Tribunal, involved the evaluation and eventual punishment of Japanese leaders for waging war as well as for the inhumane treatment of both military personnel and civilians throughout the war. Seven individuals were executed in December 1948. The most famous of the postwar trials were the Nuremberg Trials, a series of hearings held in Nuremberg, Germany, that sought to punish leaders of the Nazi Party. As a consequence of these trials, 12 individuals were hung, and many others received long prison sentences. In the end, the trials for war crimes eliminated the most radical elements of the Axis leadership, preventing them from once again gaining power in their respective countries.

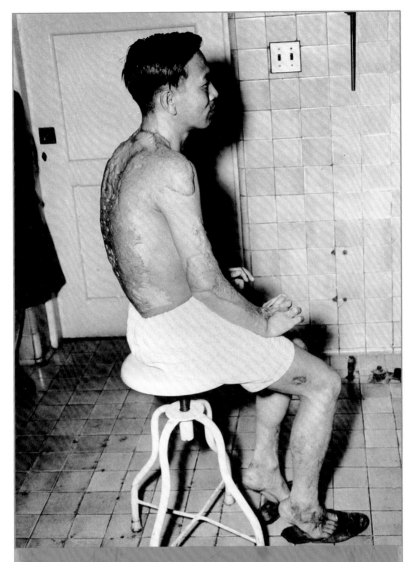

While the majority of people close to the center of the blast died immediately, those who were farther away suffered radiation and flash burns *(above)*. Symptoms of radiation sickness did not arise until several days after the bombing and more people began to die from its effects. Those who survived the bomb, the resulting burns, and radiation sickness still had long-term health problems in later years.

Out of the war came a new world order. Clearly, the Axis powers of Germany, Italy, and Japan suffered greatly, both politically and socially. Many of the privileges associated with free countries were denied, and they would all require massive rebuilding efforts. To this end, the Allied nations formed the United Nations, in San Francisco, California, in 1945. Its mission was to prevent the sudden expansion of non-democratic interests worldwide. In 1947, U.S. Secretary of State George Marshall created the European Recovery Program (better known as the Marshall Plan), which gave $13 billion in aid for the reconstruction of Western European countries that had suffered damage to their respective economies. Germany was effectively split in half, with the Americans, French, and British controlling one zone and the Soviets controlling the other. The Soviets also seized control of many nations within Eastern and Central Europe. Japan was controlled by the United States and was forced to relinquish the territory of Korea, half to the United States and half to the Soviets.

But the Axis countries were not the only nations to emerge from the war in a weakened state. France and England were forced to relinquish many of their colonies, such as India and Indochina. The Dutch colony of Indonesia gained independence as well. China reaped huge benefits. Many of the treaties imposed by imperialist nations in the past were torn up, and China formed an independent government. Because England and France had been so depleted, both in terms of the colonies they lost and the damage that was done to their economies and infrastructures, they no longer loomed as dominant nations in the Western world. In their place, the United States emerged as the preeminent world power that promoted democracy.

Perhaps as important as the reorganization of global powers, World War II taught people a great deal about politics and the destructive legacy of deterministic dictators. There were, in fact, countries where populations could be seduced by aggressive politicians who promised to deliver power and glory. The failure of the world's democratic nations to act preemptively against these menaces before they could build strength to sustain their threats was a tough pill to swallow. It was a hard lesson for the Americans especially. Pearl Harbor and the aggression of Adolf Hitler demonstrated to the Americans that they could not go on with their isolationist policies. From that point on, they would have to take a leading role in world politics.

THE NUCLEAR THREAT

Perhaps the most important and influential product of World War II was the nuclear bomb. As the bomb was developed, many scientists involved with the project expressed serious reservations about the effort. Led by the Danish physicist Niels Bohr, they attempted to convince world leaders that the atomic bomb should be shared with the Soviets. They argued that by denying the Soviets this technology, they would create an arms race that may eventually lead to massive, mutual destruction. These scientists were ignored by President Truman's administration, which saw a great advantage in nuclear superiority.

The predictions of the body of scientists turned out to be on target. In the years immediately following the war, the United States found itself fighting a global war of territory against the Communist Soviet Union. Although the two world powers never fought face to face, they were pitted against each other as they supplied other warring countries with financial backing and weapons. As the conflicts transpired, the United States and the Soviet Union began a nuclear arms race that would last 40 years. Each country built bigger, more powerful bombs. The United States created a hydrogen bomb that was 500 times more powerful than the atomic bomb that destroyed Hiroshima. In turn, the Soviet Union developed bombs more than 1,000 times more powerful.

The trend then changed from the development of more powerful bombs to bombs that could travel under their own power.

Knowing the fate of the atomic bomb victims in Japan, Americans entered into a new era of fear and preparedness as the United States and the Soviet Union competed for nuclear dominance. The arms race inspired citizens to take extra steps in protecting themselves, including building bomb shelters *(above)* in their own backyards.

Both parties developed long-range missiles carrying powerful nuclear warheads. By the 1960s, the two countries held between them an explosive force equal to 1.6 million times the force of the Hiroshima bomb, enough power to destroy civilization.

In hindsight, some very influential world figures have spoken out about the nuclear bomb. These include world leaders, scientists, philosophers, writers, and musicians. Some say

United States was wrong to drop the atomic bombs on Hiroshima and Nagasaki, that the alternatives of negotiation or a ground invasion should have been more thoroughly considered. Some say the bombs were dropped in order to intimidate the Soviet Union and therefore benefit the United States in negotiations as Europe was parceled out following the war. Others contend the United States dropped the bombs simply to test them. In any case, in the modern human psyche, the shadows of Little Boy and Fat Man move not only over the ground of Hiroshima and Nagasaki but over the world.

Chronology

1939   **August 2:** Einstein's letter urges President Roosevelt to explore nuclear chain reactions.

        September 1: Hitler invades Poland.

        September 3: The British declare war on Germany.

1940   **April 9:** Hitler invades Norway and Denmark.

        May 10: Hitler invades the Netherlands, Luxembourg, and Belgium.

        June 14: The Nazis capture Paris.

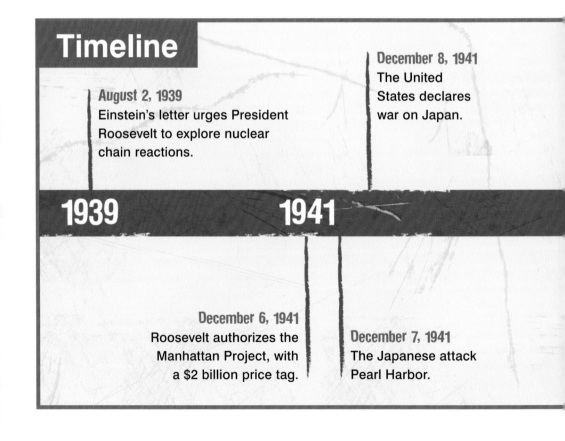

Timeline

August 2, 1939
Einstein's letter urges President Roosevelt to explore nuclear chain reactions.

December 8, 1941
The United States declares war on Japan.

1939   **1941**

December 6, 1941
Roosevelt authorizes the Manhattan Project, with a $2 billion price tag.

December 7, 1941
The Japanese attack Pearl Harbor.

September 27: Japan, Germany, and Italy sign the Tripartite Pact, creating the Axis.

1941 **June 22:** Hitler invades the Soviet Union.

December 6: Roosevelt authorizes the Manhattan Project, with a $2 billion price tag.

December 7: The Japanese attack Pearl Harbor.

December 8: The United States declares war on Japan.

1942 **April 18:** The Japanese capture Bataan.

May 8: The Battle of the Coral Sea fought.

December 2, 1942
Enrico Fermi and team produce the first controlled nuclear fission reaction in Chicago.

August 6, 1945
The *Enola Gay* drops "Little Boy" on Hiroshima.

1942 **1945**

July 16, 1945
The Trinity Test takes place at Alamogordo, New Mexico.

June 6, 1944
D-day: The Allies invade Normandy, France.

August 9, 1945
Bock's Car drops "Fat Man" on Nagasaki.

June 6: The Allies win the Battle of Midway.

December 2: Enrico Fermi and team produce the first controlled nuclear fission reaction in Chicago.

1943 **September 3:** The Allies land on the Italian mainland.

1944 **June 6:** D-day: The Allies invade Normandy, France.

August 15: The Allies retake southern France.

December 27: The Allies defeat the Germans at the Battle of the Bulge.

1945 **February 19:** U.S. Marines land on the island of Iwo Jima.

April 12: Roosevelt dies, and Harry S. Truman becomes the 33rd president of the United States.

May 7: Germany surrenders to the Allies.

July 16: The Trinity Test takes place at Alamogordo, New Mexico.

July 26: The Allies issue the Potsdam Declaration.

August 6: The *Enola Gay* drops "Little Boy" on Hiroshima.

August 9: *Bock's Car* drops "Fat Man" on Nagasaki.

August 14: Japan surrenders to the Allies.

Glossary

Allies   The 26 nations that fought against the Axis in World War II, including primarily Great Britain, France, Russia, and the United States.

anarchism   The theory or doctrine that all forms of government are undesirable and should be abolished.

Aryan   A non-Jewish Caucasian, especially of Nordic stock according to German Nazi racial theories.

atoll   An island with a circular reef surrounding a lagoon.

atomic bomb   A bomb deriving its destructive power from the release of nuclear energy.

Axis   The six nations that fought against the Allies in World War II, lead by Germany, Italy, and Japan.

blitzkrieg   Tactics employed by the Germans that emphasized precise, swift, and violent military offensives supported by intense aerial attacks.

carrier (or aircraft carrier)   A large naval vessel designed as a mobile air base, with a long, flat deck from which aircraft can take off and land at sea.

chain reaction   In physics, a series of nuclear fissions in which neutrons released by splitting one atom leads to the splitting of others.

colony   A region politically controlled by another country.

Communism   An economic system characterized by the collective ownership of property and by the organization of labor for the common advantage of all members.

democracy   A government in which the political power of a nation is spread among elected representatives of the common people.

dictator   A ruler with absolute power and unrestricted control of a government.

embargo   A prohibition by a government on certain or all trade with a foreign nation.

expansionism   A nation's practice or policy of territorial or economic expansion.

expenditure   An expense or an amount spent.

Fascism   A government in which the power of a nation is controlled by a strong, centralized government.

fission   In physics, the splitting of the nucleus of an atom into nuclei of lighter atoms, accompanied by the release of energy.

Führer   A leader, especially one exercising the powers of a tyrant.

genocide   The systematic and planned extermination of an entire national, racial, political, or ethnic group.

Hibakusha   A survivor of either of the atomic bomb attacks on Hiroshima and Nagasaki in 1945.

ideology   The body of ideas reflecting the social needs and goals of an individual, group, or culture.

isolationism   A national policy of abstaining from political or economic relations with other countries.

kamikaze   A Japanese suicide pilot from World War II trained to attack a ship by crashing his plane into it.

liberalism   A political theory founded on the natural goodness of humans and favoring civil and political liberties.

liberation   The act of setting something free, as in a nation or a group of captive people.

landing   To come to shore, unloading troops and equipment.

Nazi   A member of the National Socialist German Workers' Party, founded in Germany in 1919 and brought to power under Adolf Hitler.

neutron   An electrically neutral subatomic particle.

physicist   A scientist who specializes in the study of physics.

sanction   A measure adopted by one or more nations acting against a nation violating international law.

Socialism   A system of social organization in which the means of producing and distributing goods is owned collectively or by a centralized government that plans and controls the economy.

theoretical physics   A branch of physics in which models and abstractions, rather than experiments, are used in an attempt to understand nature.

troops   Military units or soldiers.

U-boat   A submarine of the German navy.

uranium   A toxic, radioactive metallic element that is used for nuclear weapons.

Vichy government   The puppet government of unoccupied France, set up by the Germans during World War II.

Bibliography

Alperovitz, Gar. *The Decision to Use the Atomic Bomb.* New York: Random House, 1995.

Cohen, Daniel. *The Manhattan Project.* Brookfield, Conn.: Twenty-First Century Books, 1999.

Collier, Christopher, and James Lincoln Collier. *The United States in World War II, 1941–1945.* New York: Benchmark Books, 2002.

Cooper, John W. "Truman's Motivations: Using the Atomic Bomb in the Second World War." Available online. URL: http://www.johnwcooper.com/papers/atomicbombtruman.htm. Retrieved June 2007.

"The Decision to Drop the Atomic Bomb." Harry S. Truman Library & Museum. Available online. URL: http://www.trumanlibrary.org. Retrieved August 2007.

Dowswell, Paul. *The Causes of World War II.* Chicago: Heinemann Library, 2003.

Feinberg, Barbara Silberdick. *Hiroshima and Nagasaki.* Chicago: Children's Press, 1995.

Fromm, James Richard. "Harnessing Nuclear Fission: The Story of the Atomic Bomb." Available online. URL: http://www.3rd1000.com/nuclear/cruc18.htm. Retrieved June 2007.

Harris, Nathaniel. *Hiroshima.* Chicago: Heinemann Library, 2004.

Lawton, Clive A. *Hiroshima: the Story of the First Atomic Bomb.* Cambridge, Mass.: Candlewick Press. 2004.

O'Neill, William L. *World War II: A Student Companion.* New York: Oxford University Press, 1999.

Reynoldson, Fiona. *Key Battles of World War II.* Chicago: Heinemann Library, 2001.

"The Story of Hiroshima." Hiroshima Remembered. Available online. URL: http://www.hiroshima-remembered.com/. Retrieved June 2007.

Wyden, Peter. *Day One: Before Hiroshima and After.* New York: Simon and Schuster, 1984.

Further Reading

Collier, Christopher, and James Lincoln Collier. *The United States in World War II, 1941–1945*. New York: Benchmark Books, 2002.

Grant, R.G. *Hiroshima and Nagasaki*. Austin, Tex.: Raintree Steck-Vaughn Publishers, 1998.

Harris, Nathaniel. *Hiroshima*. Chicago: Heinemann, 2004.

Langley, Andrew. *Hiroshima and Nagasaki: Fire from the Sky*. Minneapolis, Minn.: Compass Point, 2006.

O'Neill, William L. *World War II: A Student Companion*. New York: Oxford University Press, 1999.

Picture Credits

Index

About the Author

J. POOLOS has a deep interest in World War II, particularly in the development and use of atomic bombs. He has authored more than 15 books for young adults on a variety of events and historical figures.